AF269459
S.O.S.
Se están yendo las
empresas de Tijuana
Genaro
Lopez

IMMINENT COMMONS: COMMONING CITIES

SEOUL BIENNALE OF ARCHITECTURE AND URBANISM 2017

EDITED BY HELEN HEJUNG CHOI AND HYUNGMIN PAI

Notes
This book is published in conjunction
with Seoul Biennale of Architecture
and Urbanism, September 2 – November 5, 2017.

Participating cities are listed alphabetically except for Seoul and the EM/
MENA region and cities covered by
Melina Nicolaides.

Cover Image
Sekwon Ahn, *Seoul Panorama* (part),
2007. © Sekwon Ahn

Architecture and Urbanism of the Commons
Won-Soon Park, Mayor of Seoul

The Seoul Biennale of Architecture and Urbanism is taking its first step. Long dormant in the heart of our city, the Seoul Biennale, after two years of preparation, has emerged as a new cultural event for Seoul. Throughout the dizzying growth of the past half-century, architecture has served as the primary instrument of the city's development. Now, our citizens stand at the center of Seoul's urbanity. Architecture's contribution in creating a just and sustainable city is not a dream of the distant future but a reality that stands alongside our citizens. Since my inauguration as the Mayor of Seoul, I have implemented a robust range of policies such as regeneration-centered urban renovation, moving Seoul towards a pedestrian friendly city, promotion of urban manufacturing and urban farming, revitalization of local communities, and youth start-up support projects. These initiatives have brought about a new architectural paradigm, one that had long been cultivated in the everyday life of the city. The Seoul Biennale provides a milestone in the formation of architecture's new role for Seoul.

In 2013, the Seoul Metropolitan Government announced the Seoul Architecture Manifesto. It begins with the following resolution: "All architecture in Seoul is fundamentally a public asset for all of its citizens. We will work toward an architecture and urbanism of the commons that provides joy and a sense of civic pride." Based on the conviction that this consistent civic policy is the philosophical and methodological basis for addressing the impending issues of cities worldwide, *Imminent Commons* has been presented as the inaugural theme for the Seoul Biennale of Architecture and Urbanism. The Seoul Biennale presents the essentials of the urban commons, expanding beyond city policies to the what and how of the commons.

Along with Dongdaemun Design Plaza and Donuimun Museum Village, the main exhibition venues of the biennale, the historical downtown of Seoul will serve as a laboratory for discovery and experiments in policy initiatives as well as social and technological innovation. To be able to share is a blessing and a source of joy. The Seoul Biennale offers an open setting to enjoy exhibitions, participate in various projects, and engage in in-depth discussions about the future of the city. The Seoul Biennale will continue to provide a forum for cities to come together to learn, and in turn, Seoul will learn from this amazing gathering of the cities of the world.

A Biennale for Seoul, a Biennale for Architecture and Urbanism
Seung H-Sang, Chair of the Steering Board for the Seoul Biennale of Architecture and Urbanism

According to United Nation's World Urbanization Prospect report of 2014, 54% of the world's population now lives in metropolitan areas. By 2050, this percentage will increase to 86% in advanced countries, and 64% in developing nations. It is a forecast that reconfirms that the city stands at the center of the question of sustainability. With the emergence in the current era of technological networks and global inter-connections, the nation-state is losing its role as the guarantor of the safety and well-being of the individual. In recent global crises, central governments have acted less as guardians of the public good and more as instruments of narrow interests. When citizens are left to their own devices, forming solidarity becomes essential. I believe the final organization of this solidarity to be the city as a universal entity.

But what kind of city do we want? Italo Calvino stated that the true value of a city lies not in monumental buildings, but is "written in the corners of the streets, the gratings of the windows, the banisters of steps, the antennae of the lightning rods, the pole of the flags, every segment marked in turn with scratches, indentations, scrolls." Calvino is saying that the truth of the city lies in the everyday. He is asking us to break away from existing concepts of the city in order to build more humane and democratic urban structures. The city is a community always in the process of becoming, formed by anonymity and ready to tell us manifold stories. It is formed by both physical spaces—squares, parks, streets, and even gaps between buildings—and virtual spaces where strangers gather, commune, and part ways. They form the essentials of a new biennale of architecture and urbanism in Seoul.

But why Seoul? Seoul is a megacity of ten million people, a historical city that spans a millennium, and a beautiful city of mountains and streams. Located at the end of the Eurasian continent, it is a strategic point that connects the continent to the Pacific region and beyond. Destroyed under Japanese imperialism and the Korean War, the capital of what was once the world's poorest country has grown to become a global economic power. However, in the process, by indiscriminately absorbing Western capital and culture, this magnificent city lost its identity. It hurriedly erected a modernist shell as it passively incorporated itself into a global system. Nature and history, however, do not disappear: they are the powerful forces of the living city. Seoul is now energetically moving to reconstruct its identity. There is another great factor that will affect Seoul's future transformation: the unification of Korea that many say lies in the not too distant future, and which would inevitably catapult Seoul into a new era.

As the cities of the world continue to expand, will we continue to prosper? With environmental destruction, social inequality, and urban crime, we are unable to remain optimistic about the future. We must therefore ask ourselves what is a good city? The space and structure of cities, creative development and regeneration, new building methods and technology, sustainable urban environments, city governance, and new forms of solidarity: these are the central issues of the contemporary urban generation. Seoul is a global city where these issues coalesce in both a particular and universal fashion. It is where its history and tradition, its economy and culture, its politics and ideology co-exist to form a unique landscape. It is for these reasons that the Seoul Metropolitan Government has launched a new biennale of architecture and urbanism. It is in this context that the Cities Exhibition comprises an essential part of the Seoul Biennale of Architecture and Urbanism.

Helen Hejung Choi

On October 24, 2016, the *New York Times* reported on the rapid desertification of the Tengger Desert—one of four large deserts in China. Chinese desertification is now a well-known fact acknowledged in the early 2000s. The problematic issue is that the desert is slowly pushing toward the habitable areas near major cities such as Beijing. Dust and airborne particulates that originate from the Tengger Desert move eastward to the city of Taiyuan, 600 kilometers away, Beijing (931), Tianjin (997), even Seoul (1,864). This is where the phenomenon of "Asian Dust" originates every spring, and more recently, almost all year long.

This issue begins with a dearth of water, which leads to the drying out and transformation of the land. It also leads to air pollution caused by dust from the parched earth, which leads to hazards and impacts on human lives in the cities; it is clearly a municipal problem. In this context, what kind of approach or logical thinking about this issue could be applied to understanding today's cities? We learn on a daily basis that shared resources, which had long been considered to be assured to all citizens of the commons, are no longer shared or promised forever. Cities that prospered within their safe, physically demarcated boundaries are being disturbed and exploited as they are exposed to the threats and rapid changes caused by unexpected social and historical events, such as globalization, global warming, information overload, and telecommunications technology. When confronted with such changes, we attempt to define the city rationally, within the limited frame of "what it is," but these attempts are now futile and obsolete. Instead, cities are open to new, diverse, and often vague conceptualizations, yearning for different ways of strengthening their resilience and survival. New urban phenomena are simply too abundant and complex to be determined and controlled by city planning or policies. It requires many layers of tasks and views from many angles to implement

policies. Contemporary cities are developing ideas, sometimes to break away from their boundaries and borders, and working with connections between cities, the regional links among multiple cities, and sometimes links that transcend regional limits. Cities also have conditions in which they need to reconceptualize existing urban inhabitations, negotiating the coexistence and confrontation between generations and communities that have recently emerged in our physical and social spaces. These questions and ideas indicate that we now understand cities beyond the legacy of the modern city's physical structure, and they remind us of the need to keep interconnected networks of different interests in consideration.

Our needs in cities today are directly connected to the methods and processes of city governance. Many cities are already attempting to turn away from the kind of centralized, top-down municipal administrative systems that are directed by a small number of managers who implement city policies. Instead, cities today are adopting cooperative mechanisms that involve the participation of a network of interest groups that have different knowledge bases, backgrounds, and life experiences. The shift from top-down systems to more collaborative processes has allowed the participation of more citizens, who are capable of different levels of understanding of the complex and newly emerging aspects of the city. In these new processes of governance, the operation of city and governing structures becomes more horizontal. We all qualify as citizens—a group that makes decisions about both direct and indirect urban practices.

Commoning Cities asks questions about the current state and near-term future of cities around the world through the lenses of public initiatives, projects, and thematic urban narratives. Cities are looking for new possibilities that will help them survive within new systems of public administration and municipal governance in the future. The coping strategies of cities, with regard to rapid urbanization, scarcity of public resources, and privatization of the commons among others, will be examined through diverse spectrums of focused installations. These installations are a means of observation, contemplation, opportunity, experimentation, and imagination about the value of the public and the commons that is very specific to each city, yet equally capable of addressing questions shared by all cities. The objective of this exhibition is to share and make sense of various approaches to our theme, *Imminent Commons*, from the perspective of world cities and to explore possibilities and opportunities that have yet to be revealed.

The installations of *Commoning Cities* include two points of departure—one that draws an overview of the changing status of the cities, and another that focuses on place-oriented narratives. Overviews act as a "prologue" that encompasses past and present observations of the cities, from the history of modern city planning, to data visualizations, to creative civic engagements. Place-oriented presentations discuss the cities according to themes—such as current issues, specific projects, or public initiatives—that are relevant to the current interests and stakeholders of the city. The notion of places as "cities" is not always bound by the naming of an individual city as a single location, but rather sometimes as a region of many cities that share cultural traits, or even as a group of cities with the same urban symptoms. Together, the presentations create encyclopedic knowledge about cities; this leads to the possibility of being expanded, added to, and edited. The presentations are flexible enough for certain discussions to be thickened and enlarged in scale and category.

It can be worthwhile to think of each of these projects as the city's own unique condition, from its historical, social, and cultural background, but also somehow to see how it maps onto other cities as well. Population increase (or decrease), digital culture, loss of urban production, environmental threats, climate change, disaster control, and economic inequality are issues that most cities can identify with. These are both specific and "common" questions that are relevant for all of us, not just locals or natives. These are urban questions for all cities in action and transition. There are always multiple scales and definitions to blur and complicate our conception of cities. For example, climate change threatens the entire region of the East Mediterranean/Middle-East North Africa (EM/MENA), including the cities of Alexandria and Nicosia. Although both cities are in immediate need of collective monitoring initiatives, one is more concerned with the changing water level, and the other is more involved with climate change. Athenians, by contrast, have long been fighting against the privatization of water, wanting to avoid losing their most precious common good to the hands of private investors and markets. In another example, San Francisco is a place where the collective lifestyle of hippie-commune culture rose up in the 1960s; now, a revival of collective living patterns is emerging there. Rather than depending on bottom-up phenomena, there may be other ways to bring these patterns into the realm of contemporary city governance. Each city's case can be regarded as a proposal for a self-reflective network. We can easily relate San Francisco's narrative to new housing types in Seoul. We can all ask questions about definitions, borders, inhabitations, productions, and connectivities taking place in cities anytime and anywhere.

More than fifty presentations, workshops, and events engage local governments, NGOs, universities, public institutions, and civic practitioners who have an interest in and confidence in commoning cities. We gather clues that can inform new conceptions of the city. If the installations help us to reach for refreshing ideas and a new sense of the commons, we would be able to construct a new understanding of cities today. In the rapid processes of urbanization around the world, cities assert that the very future of mankind is at stake.

From the "Functional City" to "Total Function":
Planning the Modern City, 1925–1971
Annie Pedret

The history of modern town planning, as it affects contemporary approaches to the design of the city, began in the nineteenth century. The primary concerns of modern architects at the beginning of the twentieth century were the dismal living and working conditions of the industrial city, with its chaos, lack of living space, traffic, inadequate light, air, poor sanitation, lack of public space, and congestion caused by an influx of new residents from the countryside. According to the founder of the Garden City movement, Ebenezer Howard, this was accompanied by social problems of "grinding poverty," "intemperance," "restless anxiety," and "excessive toil."[1] Addressing these physical inadequacies was a key motivator for the solutions proposed by Howard and modern architects in the first quarter of the twentieth century.

According to Howard, the solution to these problems, and to the issue of centralizing power in large cities, was the Garden City. The Garden City was based on the notion of providing people with the best amenities that big cities can provide as well as with the beauties of nature. An essential feature of the resulting "town-country" was controlled speculation and self-governance in order to keep rents down and to provide the industrial worker with higher purchasing power, healthier surroundings, and more regular employment. This would be accomplished by tying rents to the annually assessed value of the land. After paying the trustees a return on investment of 4%, the excess would go to the Central Council for the creation and maintenance of public works. These Garden Cities would form a ring around the outside of the green belt surrounding the Central City to which it would be connected.

A more industrialized and top-down approach to the problems of the nineteenth-century city was promoted by CIAM (International Congress of Modern Architecture, 1928–1959), an important organization for discussion and debate on modern architecture and town planning. CIAM organized ten international meetings over the course of its history, five before World War II and five after. While the ethical premise of the organization remained the same, its priorities, methods, and approaches adjusted to changes in historical and local circumstances.

The ethical premise of modern architecture, as stated in CIAM's founding document, the "La Sarraz Declaration" (1928) from the CIAM 1 congress, was that modern architects must "morally and materially" respond to the conditions of the "present time." Their aim for a "new conception of architecture" was that it must "satisfy the spiritual, intellectual, and material demands of present-day life."[2] This would be accomplished, they stated, by linking architecture with "economic efficiency" not as "maximum commercial profit," but in terms of a means of production that minimized "working effort." That method of work was rationalization and standardization.

Although one stated aim of CIAM was to address the spiritual and intellectual demands of people, its focus was almost entirely on satisfying their physical needs. Over the next four congresses CIAM explored this aim through a series of investigations into assembly-line methods of construction in order to address the problem of lowering rents for low-income earners. This was accomplished through increasing scale: "minimum subsistence" (or "Existenzminimum") housing that was responsive to solar orientation at CIAM 2 (1929), the rational lot development of low-, medium-, and high-rise buildings at CIAM 3 (1930), the Functional City at CIAM 4 (1933), and case studies of the Functional City at CIAM 5 (1937).

The Functional City, which would be CIAM's most important theory through the influence of Le Corbusier, promoted dividing

1.
Ebenezer Howard, *Garden Cities of Tomorrow* (London: Swan Sonnenschein, 1902), 13.

2.
CIAM, "La Sarraz Declaration," in Ulrich Conrads, *Programs and Manifestoes on 20th-Century Architecture* (Cambridge, MA: MIT Press, 1971), 109.

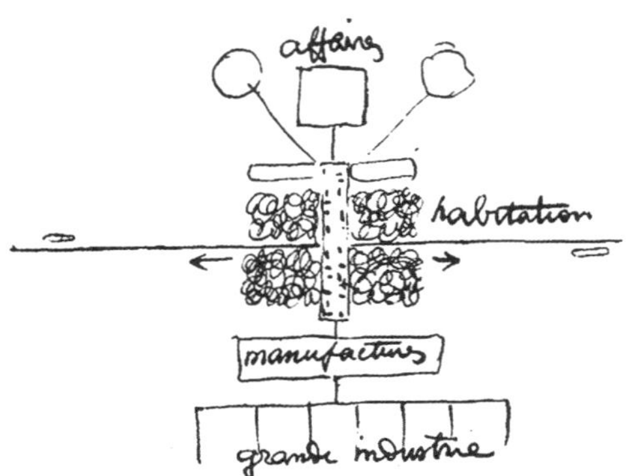

Figure 1. Le Corbusier, functional zoning diagram for the Ville Radieuse, 1935. Source: Le Corbusier, *La Ville Radieuse*, Boulogne, Seine: Éditions de L'Architecture d'Aujourd'hui, 1935. © FLC-ADAGP

the city into "autonomous" districts according to the daily functions of living-dwelling, work, recreation, and transportation. Le Corbusier expressed this concept in formal terms with sixteen display boards illustrating his Ville Radieuse project, which he brought to CIAM 3, but which he did not present. This project proposed that the solution to the problems of the chaos of the industrial city was to place intellectual work at the top, residential areas in the middle, and manufacturing, warehouses and heavy industry at the bottom (figure 1). It was a static geometric plan for a tabula rasa site with no contingency for growth or change, and it presupposed a socially stratified society with the intellectuals at the "head" and the workers located at the "bowels." This model of "high-rise towers-in-the-park" would keep cities compact, provide residents with the advantages of collectively shared recreational facilities, and ensure residents direct contact with the sky, trees, light, and "exact air." Space between the high-rise towers would also reduce the vulnerability of cities to the menace of air raids.

Gropius began to question the economic justifications of this approach to planning as early as CIAM 3 by introducing the concept that modern architects ought to also take into account the psychological idea social demands of people. At CIAM 4 and CIAM 5 congresses the limits of an analytical planning method were also discussed. At CIAM 5, Polish architect Szymon Syrkus argued that while a rational method provided a synthetic

harmony of space, the modern city should also admit the need for an approach that went beyond the analytical rationalism of dividing the city by function. He went on to assert that architects should take into account demographics and their projected change over time, as well as the interests and changing needs of inhabitants; they should acknowledge that cities do not exist in isolation but in relation to the region around them and to national context.[3] The Dutch CIAM members were skeptical of the functional city's premise, concerned that its promotion of centrally coordinated land management would lead to the collectivization of landed property; Italian CIAM members had doubts about the failure of the functional city to take into account the city's historical sections.[4] Impervious to these concerns, Le Corbusier and the French CIAM group ASCORAL would develop the epistemological framework for the functional city in the form of the CIAM Grid, which formed part of the invitation to the CIAM 7 congress in Bergamo, Italy (1949), as a means of ensuring that architects would think about the city in terms of the four functions.

With the outbreak of World War II, CIAM congresses came to a halt, but the British got busy laying out the groundwork for planning initiatives to be implemented after the end of the war. Unlike the scientific approach promoted by CIAM, they took a more regional, decentralized, and community-centered approach to addressing the problems of London's rampant growth, incoherent architectural development, traffic congestion, inadequate housing conditions, lack and poor distribution of public open space, and entangled dwelling and work functions.[5] Both the County of London Plan (1943), prepared for the London

3.
Szymon Syrkus, "Rapport no. 3 Cas d'Application Régions et Campagnes," in *Logis et Loisirs, 5e Congrès CIAM Paris 1937* (Nendeln: Kraus Reprint, 1980), 46.

4.
Dutch Group, "Propositions du Groupe Hollandais pour compléter les principes de Le Corbusier," *Logis et Loisirs*, 78. Auke Van der Woud, *Het Nieuwe Bouwen internationaal/international: CIAM Volkshuisvesting, Stedebouw: Housing, Town Planning* (Delft: Delft University Press; Otterlo: Rijksmuseum Kröller-Muller, 1983), 71.

5.
Pauline van Roosmalen, "London 1944: Greater London Plan," in *Mastering the City: North-European Town Planning 1900–2000*, eds. Koos Bosma and Helma Hellinga (Rotterdam: NAi Publishers; The Hague: EFL Publications, c. 1997), 258.

County Council by Sir Patrick Abercrombie and John Henry Forshaw, and the Greater London Plan (1944) by Abercrombie, commissioned by the Ministry of Town and Country Planning, conceived of London as a collection of zones with varying functions that had either been inadequately separated or inadequately connected. The purpose of the first of these two plans was to sustain an interrelated system of communities that were divided into "neighbourhood units." Each community was a separate entity with its own identity and affiliations to its own schools, public buildings, shops, and open spaces. To address the problem of slums, new housing in the form of the Garden City, with a number of high blocks for single people and childless couples, would be built in a way that would reflect the new postwar reality.

The most radical aspect of the plan was to rehouse 500,000 people outside London in satellite towns at a fifty-mile (eighty-kilometer) radius from London[6] using the decentralized model of Howard's Garden City. Part of Abercrombie's concept was to create concentrated clusters of buildings with adequate distance separating them. One major point of departure for his plan was to maintain the quality of the countryside and create open spaces. The second was acknowledging the importance of cities to regional and national economies. Abercrombie's planning concept featured four concentric zones: a high-density "inner city" zone of the County of London; a second ring of lower-density residential suburbs; a "green belt" surrounding the suburban ring, which acted as a buffer between the expansion of London and regional communities; and the outermost ring of adjacent counties, which would allow for the decentralization of people and industry by building new towns in undeveloped areas or by adapting existing settlements to function as town centers. These new towns were not very large, and each had its own character and function, employment opportunities, and balanced composition of population. They would be connected to London by means of five county beltways and ten radial roads.[7] This plan paved the way for the founding of twenty new towns in Britain between 1946 and 1950; the emphasis on com-

munities, and their relationship to one another, is a theme that would be elaborated by younger CIAM members Alison and Peter Smithson. This model of decentralization has influenced the development of megacities like Seoul.

World War II changed everything—politically, socially, economically and culturally. CIAM reconvened in Bridgwater, England at CIAM 7 (1947) to take stock of the vastly changed circumstances and to reaffirm the aims of CIAM: "to work for the creation of a physical environment that will satisfy man's material and emotional needs," but with an emphasis that modern architects also needed to stimulate their "spiritual growth."[8]

What was meant by "spiritual growth" or "spiritual needs" was never defined by CIAM or its individual members, but it clearly did not refer to the spiritual in religious or theological terms. Rather, it was a possible means to "humanize" modern architecture by acknowledging the fullness of human reality beyond the physical realm.[9] It was closer to Michel Foucault's use of the word as a way of gaining access to a fuller range of human needs—both physical and spiritual—that take many forms and change with time and circumstance.

For CIAM members, the spiritual was the antidote to contemporary ills, such as the "dispiriting absence of soul/spirit from which mechanized society was suffering,"[10] according to Le Corbusier. The spiritual also addressed the dissatisfaction with the new towns and the inadequate results of the problematic mechanics of urbanism in the functional city that had "nothing to do with spirit,"[11] according to British CIAM member Peter

6.
Municipal Dreams, "The County of London Plan, 1943: 'This New World Foreshadowed,'" July, 15 2014. https://municipaldreams. wordpress.com/2014/07/15/the-county-of-london-plan-1943/.

7.
Van Roosmalen, "London 1944: Greater London Plan," 258.

8.
CIAM, "Re-Affirmation of the Aims of CIAM," in *A Decade of New Architecture, ed. Sigfried Giedion* (Zurich: Girsberger, 1951), 17.

9.
Clare O'Farrell, "Key Concepts," 2007. http://www.michel-foucault. com/concepts.

10.
Le Corbusier, "Discourse de Le Corbusier au Vième Congrès CIAM. Séance de l'Assemblée Générale sur l'Expression Architectural," September 15, 1947, Bakema Archive, Het Nieuwe Instituut, Rotterdam (hereafter BA HNI).

11.
Peter Smithson, "Notes of Meeting of MARS Group CIAM 10 Sub-Committee," April 23, 1954, written by John Voelcker and Trevor Dannatt, May 1954, BA HNI

Smithson, and it "lets through most of what goes to make life,"[12] according to Dutch CIAM member Aldo van Eyck. It also was a way to deal with the problem faced by the younger CIAM members: solving the technical problem of building for "quantity" while maintaining the identity or "quality" by paying attention to the parts of something within a whole and the particularity of individuals and their communities and cultures.[13]

This discourse about "spiritual needs" was a reaction against their dissatisfaction with the functional city, which eventually led to the formation of a splinter group of younger CIAM members that became known as Team 10. This diverse group of architects included Peter and Alison Smithson, Aldo van Eyck, Jacob (Jaap) Bakema, and Georges Candilis, among others. While being bound by their commitment to the ethic of modern architecture—being of the present-day—they were diverse in their approaches to the postwar context. With this new set of values came a new vocabulary for developing modern architecture at mid-century; it put into practice the ethic of modern architecture, of responding to the conditions of the present day, which mass communication and transportation had made more global than ever, with other cultures and their differences closer than they had ever been before, with the conversion of wartime production to consumer goods accompanied by advertising creating more desires than perhaps there had ever been before. Team 10 members responded to this changed world using different approaches, theories, formal articulation, and personal vocabularies with the aim of meeting the spiritual needs of people.

The vocabulary of modern architecture in the 1950s and 1960s shifted from standardization, economic and productive efficiency—and from using analytical and rational thinking methods—to more humane ideals. The *needs* that modern architects were to satisfy now included aspirations, emotion, expression, aesthetics, art, poetry, growth, and change, identity, choice, "human association," belonging, community, collective life, "whole social process," "grace," "healthy vitality," "habitat," and socio-geographically integrated environments. The architectural *means* for satisfying

those spiritual needs differed among Team 10 members but included integration, "whole particular complexes," historical continuity, a conception of history that includes the present, "totalities," the "visual group," "identifying devices," "cluster," local character, relationships between people, "human association," mobility, and particular behaviors, forms, social, territorial conditions, and culture.[14] It was now about more complexity and more relationships between people and things, of particularity organized as "whole complexed" rather than standardized uniformity and universality.

The founding document for Team 10 was drafted at a meeting in Doorn, Holland, in 1954. In it they stated that the earlier method for restoring order in nineteenth-century cities, by classifying an "overwhelming variety of city activities" into four distinct functions, was inadequate for "liberating the potential" of the twentieth century. This approach, they argued, tended "to produce 'towns' in which vital human associations are inadequately expressed." This approach ought to be replaced by one that considered "every community as a particular total complex" of varying degrees of complexity and differing kinds of human association.[15]

The congress that best expresses the diverse contexts and approaches confronting modern architects was the last congress, CIAM '59, at Otterlo, Holland, in 1959. Organized entirely by Team 10 members, the presentations ranged from Ralph Erskine's Ecological Arctic Town project, to photos of the Dogon tribe of Mali, West Africa, by Herman Haan, to the hotly contested functional-historicist debates about both BBPR's Torre Velasca in Milan and Giancarlo de Carlo's housing project in Matera, Italy, to the proto-mega-struc-

12.
Aldo van Eyck to Alison and Peter Smithson, c. September 1954. BA HNI

13.
Aldo van Eyck, "Conclusion of Sub-Commission Meetings on 20 and 21st of July 1953," in "Le Logis dans le Unité d'Habitation," BA HNI.

14.
Annie Pedret, "From 'Spirit of the Age' to the 'Spiritual Needs' of People," in *Re-Humanizing Architecture: New Forms of Community, 1950–1970*, vol. 1 of *East West Central: Re-Building Europe, 1950–1990*, eds. Ákos Moravánszky and Judith Hopfengärtner (Berlin, Basel: Birkhäuser; de Gruyter, 2016).

15.
Jacob Bakema, Aldo van Eyck, Sandy van Ginkel, Peter Smithson, John Voelcker, Hans Hovens-Greve, "Statement on Habitat," Doorn, Holland, January 1954, BA HNI.

Figure 2. Fumihiko Maki, group form diagram, 1964. Source: Fumihiko Maki, *Investigations in Collective Form*, Washington University, St. Louis, 1964; *Nurturing Dreams: collected essays on architecture and the city* (Cambridge, Mass.: MIT Press, 2008). Photo courtesy of Maki & Associates.

turalism of Louis I. Kahn's parking structures in his proposal for traffic in downtown Philadelphia. Team 10 thinking would become the theoretical basis for the work of individual Team 10 members, that resonated with attendees, like De Carlo and Kenzo Tange, who thought along similar lines. When De Carlo attended the Otterlo meeting he was already tackling the problem of the dissatisfaction of people with the "functional" approach to modern architecture as he was finishing the first phase of his project for the Università di Urbino. Instead of designing an idealized city on a *tabula rasa* site as proposed by Le Corbusier in his Ville Radieuse projects, De Carlo spent the first eight years of the project (1952-1960) developing the core premise of studying the "complex system of physical and spatial phenomena" in which the residents of Urbino had been harmoniously living.[16] He would continue to develop a long-term plan based on establishing a relationship between the university and the historic fabric of the old town of Urbino over the next five decades. Tange, who was not a member of team 10, would return to Tokyo after the Otterlo meeting to become associated with the Metabolist group, established in 1960. Although the members were diverse in their approaches, they shared a vision of designing future cities capable of continuous growth and change. In contrast to the static nature of Le Corbusier's plans for the modern city that were understood as an ordering of autonomous component parts, the Metabolists conceived of the city in biological terms as being like a living organism that depended on its metabolism for maintaining

its essential processes of life.[17] Metabolism, or "total function"—that is, the material and energy exchange between the organism and the exterior world—maintained the harmonious functioning of all the attributes of an organism—physical, mental, and spiritual. Tange would develop a "mega-structuralist" approach to ensure the growth of the city, while fellow Metabolist Fuhimiko Maki developed the notion of "group form"—a type of spatial organization that results from adding individual elements sequentially to create a "non-hierarchical collective form," or group, whose elements share the same character, and that encourages cumulative growth (figure 2).[18] Team 10 thinking also resonated with Robert Venturi's *Complexity and Contradiction in Architecture* (1966), and with post-structuralist thought developing in the culture at large.

A conceptual history of modern town planning through the lens of CIAM and Team 10 provides the background to concepts that are not new to architectural and urban discourse, but which become renewed by virtue of the fact that they are now addressing new problems in entirely new circumstances—in the first decades of the twenty-first century, these are rapid growth and change and its repercussions on what is now is no longer the "commons," but "imminent commons."

16.
Luca Molinari, "The Spirits of Architecture: Team 10 and the Case of Urbino," in *Team 10, 1953–1981: In Search of a Utopia of the Present*, eds. Max Risselada and Dirk van den Heuvel (Rotterdam: NAi, 2005), 302.

17.
Zhongjie Lin, *Kenzo Tange and the Metabolist Movement: Urban Utopias of Modern Japan* (London and New York: Routledge, 2010), 22.

18.
Ibid., 113.

Aerial view of Mexico City, XIII, 2006. © Pablo López Luz

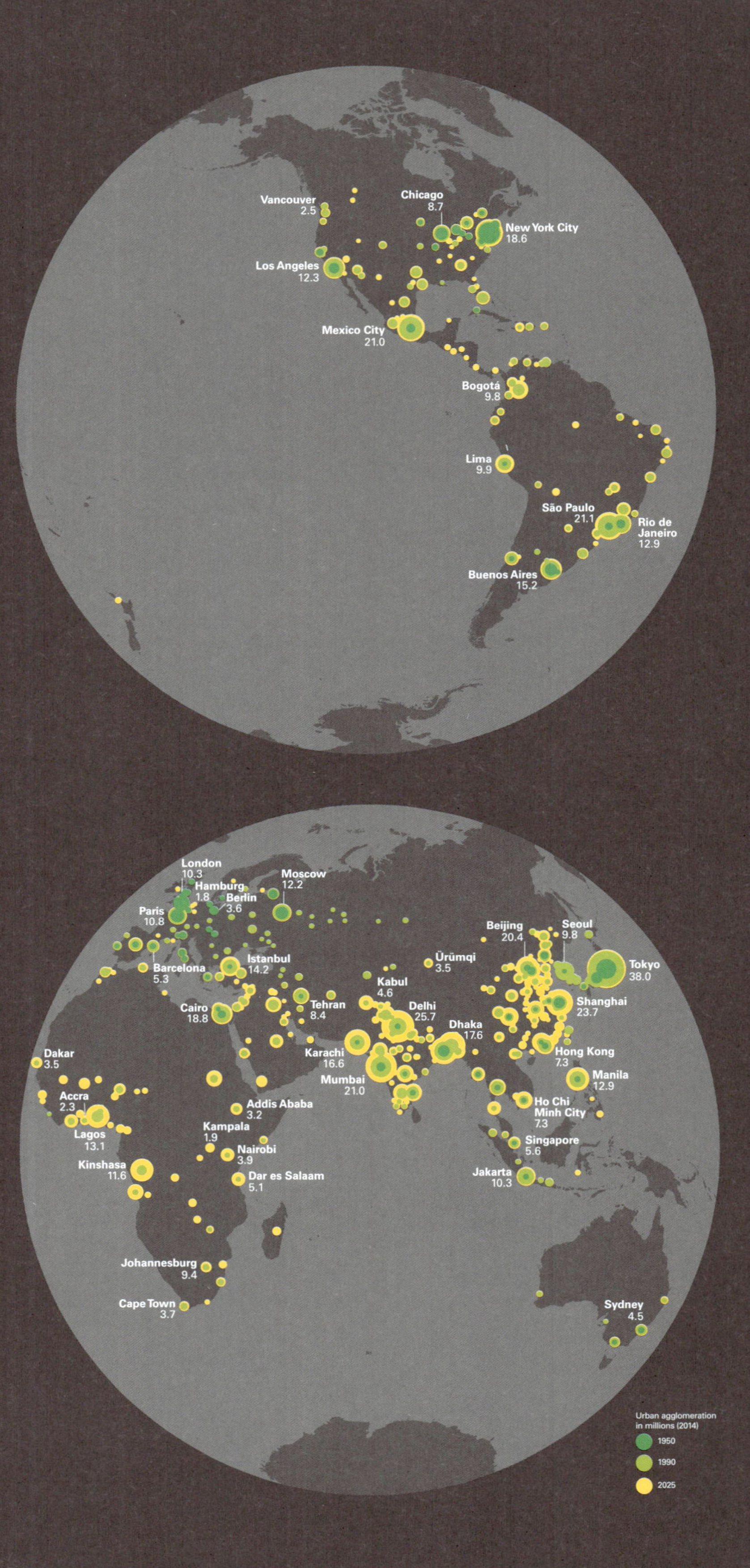

Vancouver
2.5
Chicago
8.7
New York City
18.6
Los Angeles
12.3
Mexico City
21.0
Bogotá
9.8
Lima
9.9
São Paulo
21.1
Rio de
Janeiro
12.9
Buenos Aires
15.2
London
10.3
Hamburg
1.8
Moscow
12.2
Berlin
3.6
Paris
10.8
Beijing
20.4
Seoul
9.8
Barcelona
5.3
Istanbul
14.2
Ürümqi
3.5
Tokyo
38.0
Cairo
18.8
Kabul
4.6
Tehran
8.4
Delhi
25.7
Shanghai
23.7
Dakar
3.5
Dhaka
17.6
Accra
2.3
Karachi
16.6
Hong Kong
7.3
Manila
12.9
Mumbai
21.0
Addis Ababa
3.2
Ho Chi
Minh City
7.3
Lagos
13.1
Kampala
1.9
Nairobi
3.9
Singapore
5.6
Kinshasa
11.6
Dar es Salaam
5.1
Jakarta
10.3
Johannesburg
9.4
Cape Town
3.7
Sydney
4.5
Urban agglomeration
in millions (2014)
1950
1990
2025

The Urban Age Programme, organized by LSE Cities at the London School of Economics and Deutsche Bank's Alfred Herrhausen Gesellschaft, is an international investigation of how the physical and social are interconnected in cities. The program centers on an annual conference, research initiatives, and publications. Since 2005, sixteen conferences have been held in rapidly urbanizing regions in Africa and Asia, as well as in mature urban regions in the Americas and Europe.

The program explores the way in which selected "Urban Age" cities perform in global hot spots of urbanization, revealing the complex patterns of urban growth, mobility, density, social inclusion, economic development, environmental impact, and governance structures that lie behind cities as diverse as Mexico City and Tokyo, Delhi and Johannesburg, Istanbul and London, Seoul and Addis Ababa.

In the short time span of twenty-five years, cities have grown larger and more quickly than ever before. Fishing villages have been transformed into megacities, and deserts have become urban playgrounds. The speed and scale of this transformation is unprecedented. By the middle of this century, 75% of the world's population will be living in cities.

Cities occupy less than 1% of global land, but generate over two-thirds of the world's economic output. They are the stage-sets for social opportunity and social inequality. While some cities are pioneering sustainable and imaginative solutions, many are not. New city forms are also emerging, with profound social and environmental consequences for billions of urban dwellers.

The exhibition describes the changing urban dynamics of global cities and focuses on how seven cities have changed over the last twenty-five years. It foregrounds individual narratives on how the physical environment has adapted to societal change and presents data on the urban dynamics that affect people's lives. Alongside this, Urban Age research provides a comparative overview of how cities across the world are organized, planned, and managed. It features a comparative snapshot of how different cities perform against a broad range of physical and social indicators.

The world's urban population is unevenly distributed. African and Asian cities are growing faster than ever before; the growth of Latin American cities has slowed, while those in Europe and the United States have peaked. Some cities have grasped the opportunity to plan and grow more equitably. Others have suffered sprawl and unplanned growth.

Amsterdam
Amsterdam Approach

Eric van der Kooij
City of Amsterdam, Department of Planning and Sustainability

Amsterdam has a very active planning tradition, thanks in part to the city's strong position as owner of most of its land. Current dynamics, however, pose questions about this leading role, as developments become more complex and intertwined and occur increasingly rapidly. Straightforward master planning is shifting toward a more adaptive planning approach.

Amsterdam is a city with a global appeal, with an international population and many international firms. With its three hubs (Schiphol airport, the Port of Amsterdam, and the AMS-IX internet hub), it is very well connected, making it function as an international metropolis. However, with only 845,000 inhabitants, Amsterdam is a rather small city in this international context. Growth in Amsterdam is strongly linked to the growth and development of the metropolitan region. The housing and labor markets, regional traffic system, metropolitan landscape, and the energy transition away from fossil fuels are all administered regionally.

In recent years the city has grown rapidly in terms of inhabitants, jobs, and visitors. This not only makes the city prosper, but also poses potential threats, especially since opportunities for expanding the city are limited. Growth can lead to extreme crowding, longer waiting lists (for example, for social housing), higher rents, smaller houses, longer journey times, and greater social divisions and inequality. It also puts pressure on mobility in general, including sanitation, energy, waste disposal, and the need for urban amenities such as parks or sport fields.

In order to overcome these challenges

Map showing the integration of interwoven aspects, such as mobility and green spaces for future transformations.

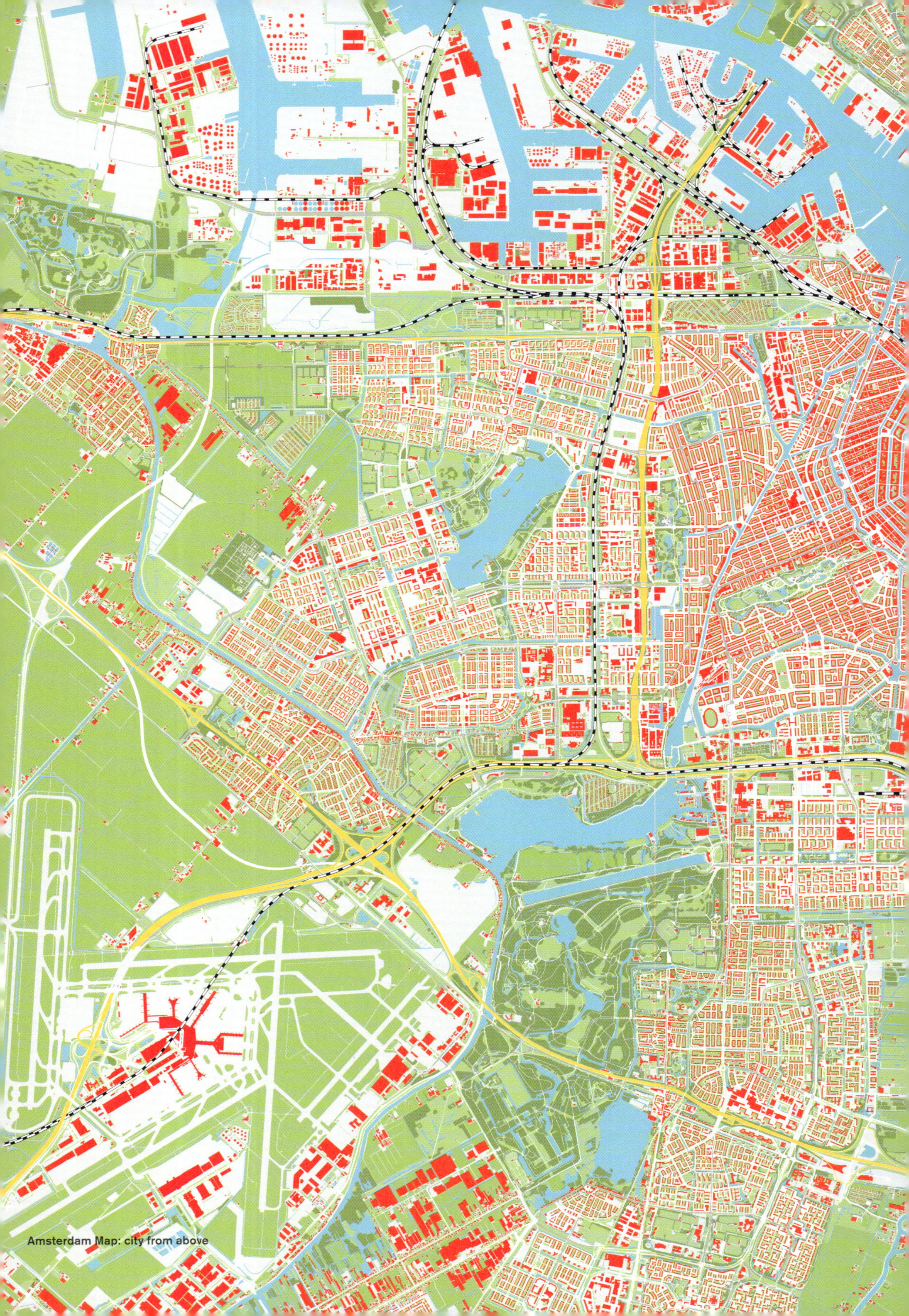

Amsterdam Map: city from above

and threats, the municipal council decided in 2016 to invest in this growth to accommodate and provide sustainable, diverse, and liveable environments for its inhabitants.

The recent economic crisis made Amsterdam realize that it should not focus on growth alone. It urges the principles of horizontal governance and flexible planning tools to adapt to future changes. Focus is shifting from quantity to quality, searching for new ways for the public to participate, co-create, and use their imaginations to design the city we want to be.

This touches on some of the most basic and fundamental questions in urban planning: Why do we plan? How do we do it? And with whom? These essentially address the qualitative aspects of growth. How can a city with a strong planning tradition and cultural and economic ambitions maintain equality, diversity, liveability, and loveability for future generations? How can we accommodate growth, while adapting or integrating new systems that require a different approach and attitude?

The exhibition highlights the need to clarify and reload the story, and it specifies what is necessary to achieve this with regard to strategies that focus on transformation, densification of existing areas, accessibility, sustainability, building communities, open and green spaces, inclusiveness, and functional diversity. After all, Amsterdam is for everybody!

The studies are put forward in constant dialogue with inhabitants, entrepreneurs, property developers, educational institutions, and public organizations using the "Amsterdam Principles" and leading to a new vision of the future city.

The Amsterdam Principles are presented at the "Poldertable." The table holds the nine principles, which address how to organize a successful dialogue, described as the art of "polderen." It focuses on the attitudes and approaches that are necessary to overcome obstacles, and on sharing common goals and solutions in the process of city making.

Bangkok
Street Food: A Common Canteen

Niramon Kulsrisombat
Urban Design Development Center (UddC)

Bangkok is well known for its food scene; in fact, CNN named it the city with best street food in the world in 2016. The vibrant images that attract the media and visitors serve their purpose in promoting tourism in the city. Behind the scenes, though, there are other dimensions of street food: it is part of local daily consumption and also contributes to the urban system itself. Here, we focus on the urban system and observe how the street food industry responds to diverse urban behavior, as it exemplifies a potential design domain that promotes an inclusive city.

Bangkok's urban conditions shape how its inhabitants live, work, and play, rather than the other way around: allowing people to shape their conditions. Over the past decade, urban sprawl has increased; more people live in the suburbs and rely on automobiles to commute to work in the city center. The limited availability of public transport and urban amenities, which cover only the city center and radial roads, limits pedestrian accessibility to everyday destinations. These built environments reflect the hustle and bustle of urban life, which makes getting around and eating more time-consuming and expensive and contributes to the high cost of living. One mechanism that enables Bangkok to accommodate diverse people is street food, affordable quick meals within walking distance. There are more than 200,000 street vendors

Street vendors in Bangkok.

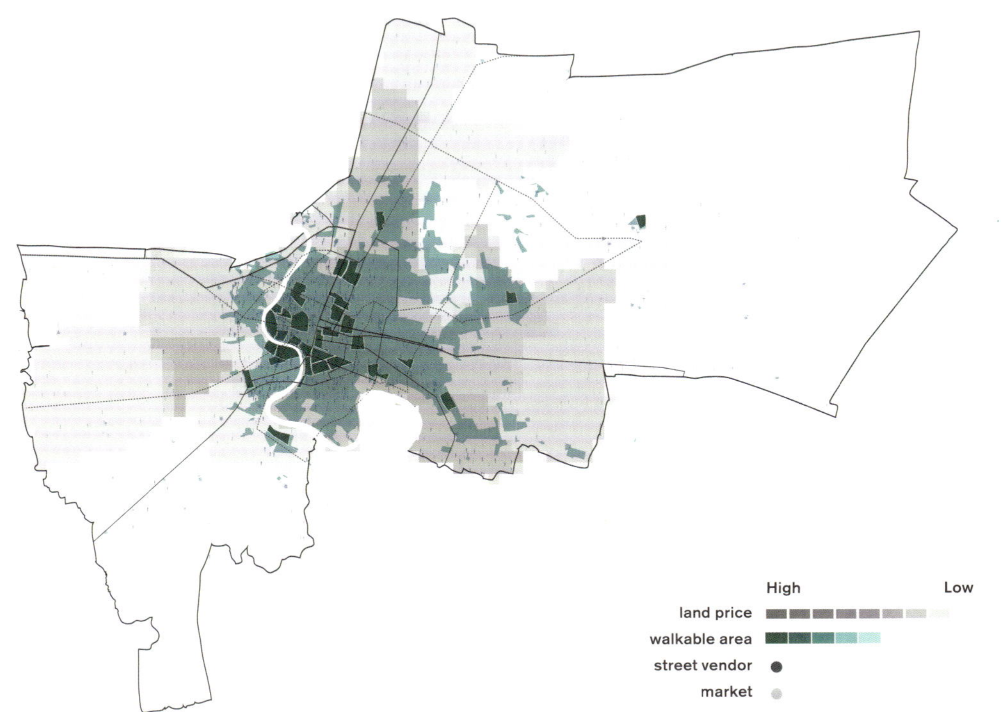

Ari-Pradipat neighborhood, the GoodWalk Thailand Project.

in Bangkok, suggesting its economic impact and relation to the urban system as a whole. Street vendors are one of the few urban elements that adjust to people's behavior.

The Goodwalk Thailand Project, a research study on public amenities and the built environment for walkability, reveals that street vendors contribute both positive and negative factors to neighborhoods. On the one hand, they promote the liveliness of the streets, but on the other hand, they create obstacles to walking. A case study of the Ari-Pradipat neighborhood—a mixed-use commercial area along a radial road, surrounded by residential clusters—offers an interesting site to observe the flow of people and street-vending activities. The key finding was that street vendor placement follows where people walk and where they stop at nodes or landmarks. From the analysis of space syntax, this correlates with the most integrated street. The variety of street vendors respond to different customer demands during the day, especially when the dynamic of the neighborhood is enhanced by its mixed-use function. The relationship between street vendors and their customers leads to social inclusion and creates a sense of place.

In conclusion, the observation that street food is a responsive mechanism within the city yields insight and knowledge and serves as a potential design domain that encourages an inclusive city. The next question is: if street food is seen as a common amenity, what kind of physical infrastructure and management is required?

The exhibition is divided into three parts. The first part, "Bangkok in Common," gives an overview of Bangkok's spatial configuration and the urban conditions that shape how inhabitants live, work, and play in the city. Supported by a series of city-level maps that display key information on demographics, land use, transportation networks, and public amenities, information on policies and the socio-economic aspects of street vendors is presented. The second part, "Street Food as Responsive Mechanism," presents a case study of the Ari-Pradipat neighborhood, a mixed-use commercial area along a radial road with intensive street-vendor activities. The findings about the responsive nature of street vendors are displayed in diagrams of pedestrian flow, walkability index, street-vendor location, public amenities, and a collection of images. The third part, "An Urban Amenity for an Inclusive City," opens a discussion on a key question: if street food is seen as a common amenity, what kind of physical infrastructure and management is required? Since street vendors relate to the urban system at a site-specific level, the challenges and suggestions need to address policy, planning, and patterns of behavior across the multi-scale levels.

Barcelona Metropolitan Area (AMB) Institute for Advanced Architecture of Catalonia (IAAC)

The soul of a city is built into its public spaces and buildings. They define the character of the shared values of a society as it builds its commons.

The Barcelona Metropolitan Area (AMB) has been working for decades to build public facilities at strategic points of its urban fabric. Public facilities provide the basic services that citizens need to live, and they are the nodal attractors in every neighborhood. Rather than letting "the market" organize basic services for citizens, we have been building a public network of facilities that includes markets, health centers, libraries, sport centers, cultural centers, auditoriums, music schools, kindergartens, elementary schools, high schools, civic centers, city councils, and innovation centers, all open to everyone. These centers are the attractors that every citizen needs; placed in dense city neighborhoods, no more than ten minutes' walk from every house.

But the metropolitan area of Barcelona is urbanized almost everywhere, and there is a lack of free space to build additional facilities that are required by citizens. That's why more and more we are building mixed-use facilities that are able to host many different functions, which creates more complex urban interactions concentrated in one spot in the same building.

The architecture of these buildings is also a key element in defining the identity of every neighborhood and district. Public buildings try not to be rare artifacts but rather good, domestic buildings, open to the community, that everyone can understand and use. The public spaces attached to them are places where families and friends can play, interact, cohabit together, and sometimes use for public events. That's why when making facilities that concentrate functions—like a market, a kindergarten, and a library in the same building,

Mercè Rodoreda Library. Authors: Amb (Carlos Llinàs), Location: Sant Joan Despí, 2011. © Photo by Aleix Bagué

Baix Llobregat Regional Archive & Mas Lluí Civic Center. Authors: AMB (dataAE + Xavier Vendrell Studio), Location: Sant Feliu de Llobregat, 2011. © Photo by Adrià Goula

or a primary school, a civic center, a library, and an elderly center in another—the city starts to function in a different way.

A building with mixed use allows the public to be there for a longer time, generating a more dynamic and intensive use of the public spaces in the building. A mixed-use building also allows this spot to be used by different generations of citizens, creating a richer inter-generational use of public spaces and buildings. So we are creating *Mixed Use, Mixed Time, Mixed People*.

The Barcelona Metropolitan Area (AMB) presents in the Seoul Biennale of Architecture and Urbanism a selection of some of its mixed-use public facilities via drawings and videos that show how life is happening in a very natural way in these buildings and the public spaces attached to them. If the city of the future is a metropolis of neighborhoods, these public spaces and buildings are the core of what we understand as urbanity.

Beijing
Code City

Code City Research Team
Tongji University

If the modern city is a game of solid volumes and hollow spaces, the zoning code for the city is like the rules for Go. The story of zoning is the history of how urban planners learned to regulate competition for access to natural resources, such as natural light, fresh air, and open views. The city of New York was the first to pass a modern zoning code, the 1916 Zoning Resolution, in order to harness its feverish urban growth at the beginning of the twentieth century. The 1916 Zoning Resolution underwent major revision in 1961, introducing the concept of "incentive planning": this encourages private developers to provide "privately owned public spaces" to the public in return for allowing extra floor area to be built. Both the 1916 and 1961 Zoning Resolutions shaped the iconic streetscape and skyline of New York City.

In China, Detailed Regulatory Planning, a mix of socialist urban planning and western zoning codes, is the major instrument that planning agencies use to balance the interests of the capital, the public, and the state. Detailed Regulatory Planning inherits Soviet-style planning practices and is deeply grounded in the mentality of the planned economy. Hence, inspired by Hong Kong's leasehold sales, the land auction system was established in the Post-Reform Era (1978 to the present); in this system, urban land is allocated for leasehold sales by local officials. The land auction system preselects developers with higher solvency, who are more capable of developing a large tract of land with minimum infrastruc-

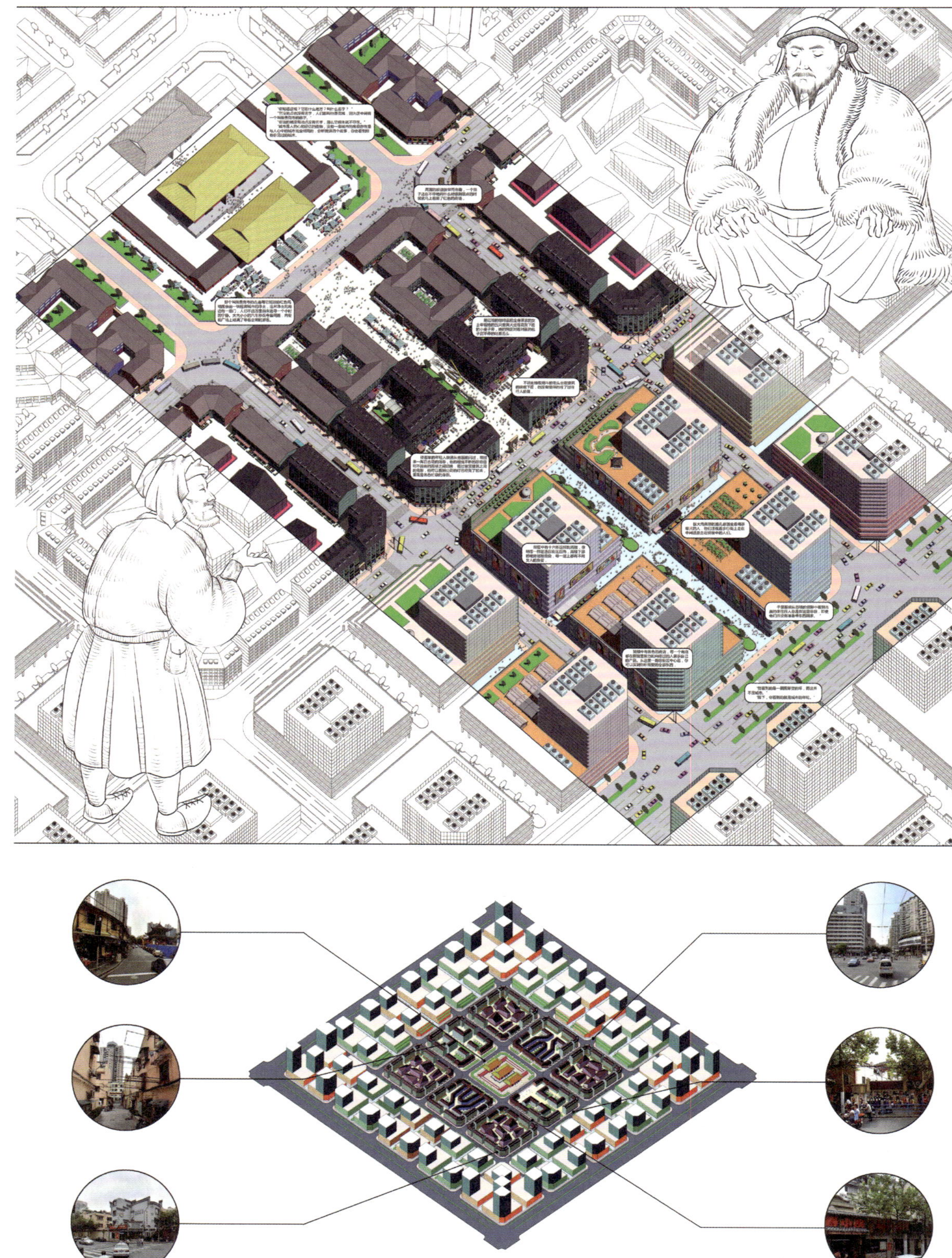

Two "Fictopian" Cities: Turning Urban Stories to Urban Rules. © *Code City* research team

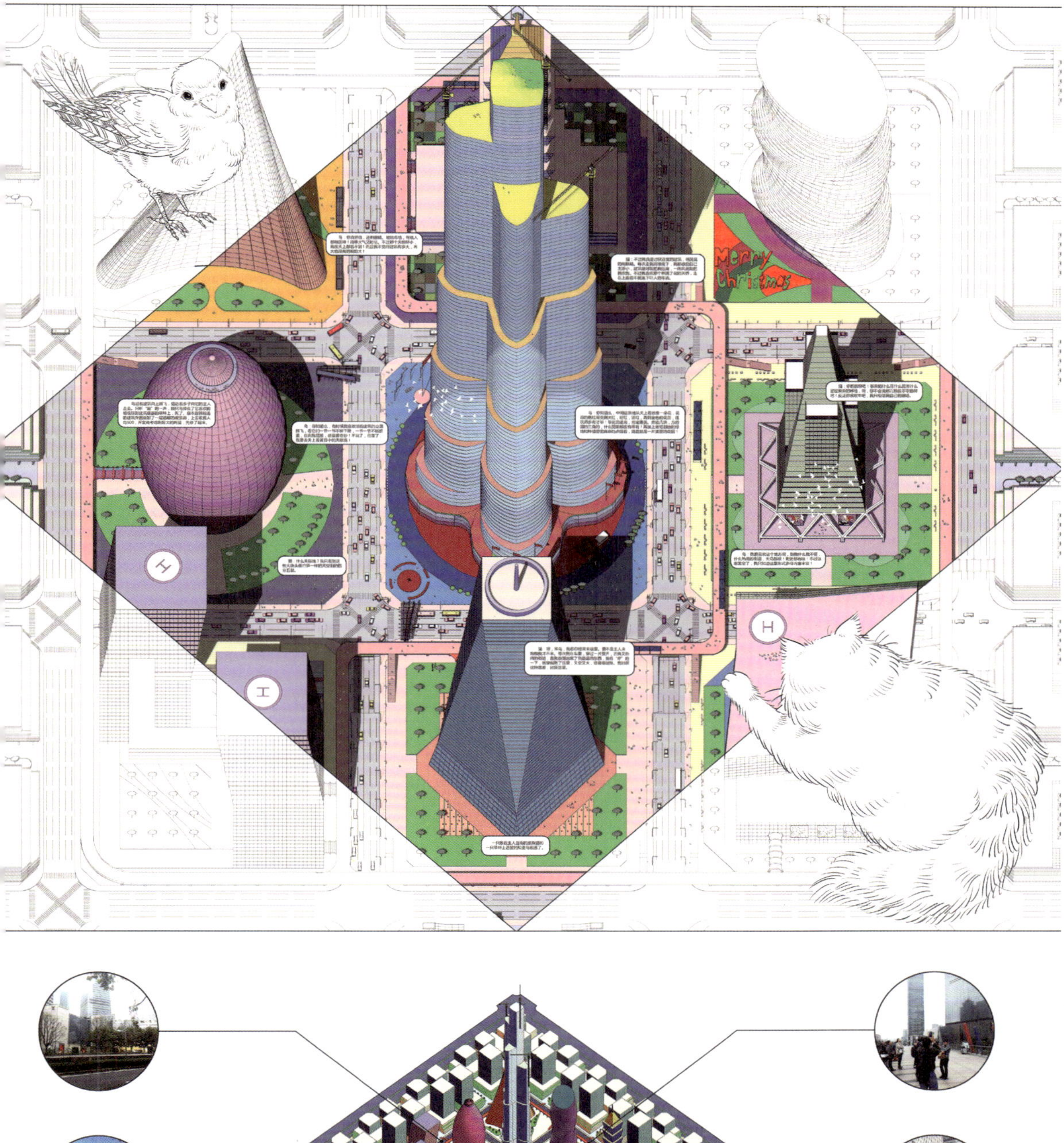

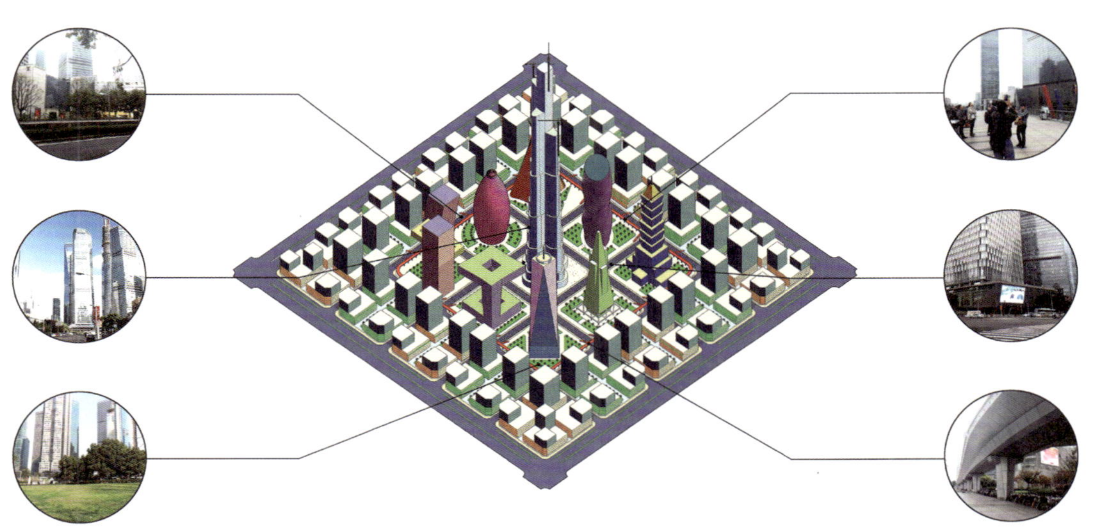
Merry Christmas

tural investment from local municipal governments. Beijing, as well as other Chinese megacities, is heavily subject to Detailed Regulatory Planning and the land auction system. In the past three decades under this regime, a generic development pattern, featuring superblocks, expressways, high-rise towers, and shopping malls, has been formed. In this sense, our project explores and critiques the (in)ability of zoning codes to guide the urbanization of China. The objective of this exhibition is to show the internal paradox of China's planning system and to demonstrate hypothetical urban forms when these zoning codes are changed, compromised, or upgraded.

Through visualization/mapping, narrative collage, transcultural studies, and educational games, we would like to critique the existing zoning codes in China and exhibit alternative urban morphological scenarios based on a hypothetical manipulation of zoning codes and building regulations. The main body of the exhibition tells four urban "fables" in a typical Chinese context. These fables feature prototypical urban forms and expose the tensions between the public and the private, the general and the specific, and the privileged and the unprivileged. Each story will focus on a specific function of the zoning codes, such as land use planning, density, massing, or building design guidelines.

Starting with personal narratives from fictional protagonists, these stories will eventually lead to a comprehensive critique of the existing zoning codes. Inspired by the urban massing studies of New York architectural delineator Hugh Ferriss in the 1930s and 1940s, and employing visualization tools, we seek to demonstrate the enormous impact that zoning codes in Chinese megacities can have on urban forms and consequently on everyday life. Despite its history as a commonly used apparatus for planners for over a century, the invisible relationship between zoning codes and urban forms remains an "urban legend" for laypeople as well as for many architects and urban designers. People might be aware of the distinctions between cities in different parts of the world (typical building types, development intensity, street grid patterns,

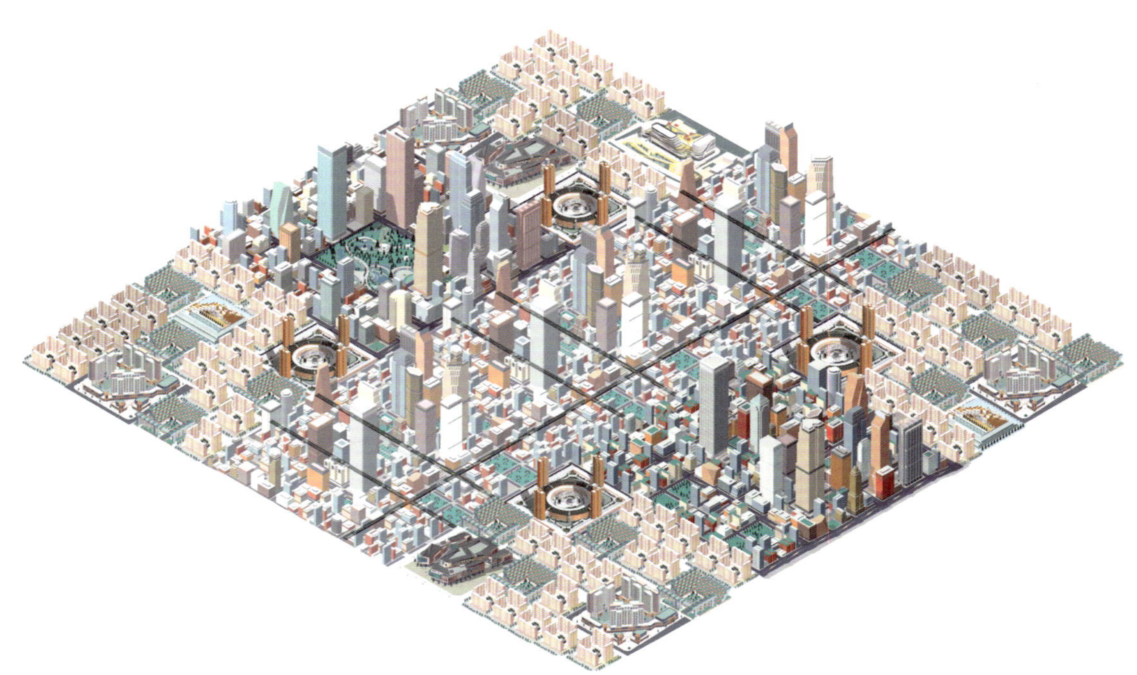

A Panoramic City Collage of Code-Driven Buildings. © *Code City* research team

urban fabric, etc.) but are certainly unaware of the underlying zoning processes and their impact on cities. People should be more informed about the effect of zoning codes and a culture of "code manipulation" in the history and practice of architecture and urbanism.

Berlin
Die Laube in the City Garden: Architecture as a Trigger Towards a Co-produced City
Quest | An Urban Laboratory
(Christian Burkhard, Florian Köhl)

Prinzessinnengärten was founded in the summer of 2009 on Moritzplatz in Kreuzberg in the heart of Berlin. Conceived as a pilot project for the development of new forms of self-managed green space, the former wasteland was transformed by volunteers into a thriving urban garden. As a nonprofit community project, the Prinzessinnengärten is open to the public. Although a wide variety of vegetables and herbs grow there, the garden's main focus is educational and social activities, not food production; moreover, the garden offers open courses on subjects like organic agriculture, biodiversity, beekeeping, and upcycling, among others. The garden is financed by a vegetarian restaurant and a gardening workshop, which builds community gardens for schools and other institutions.

Die Laube (The Arbor) is a self-built, three-story, ten-meter-high, modular wooden structure in the Prinzessinnengärten. It was developed and designed by Quest (Christian Burkhard and Florian Köhl) in collaboration with Marco Clausen, one of the founders of the Prinzessinnengärten. Construction started in 2015; the building process is continuous. To erect *Die Laube*, no cranes are used and no knowledge of building construction is needed. More than 100 volunteers have invested 10,000 working hours to make the project become a reality. The act of building has created a common purpose. So, in extrapolation of the principles of community gardening, *Die Laube*'s modularly built structure brings about an architecture geared toward a practical discussion of social, economic, and ecological issues related to the built environment. It posits itself as an infrastructure for the process of social learning.

Through its experimental construction, and as a new locality, *Die Laube* also reinforces connections between local social initiatives, crafts schools, environmental NGOs, the Prinzessinnengärten's own educational platform ("Neighbourhood Academy"), professional associations, private companies, and academic institutions. This has led to a local discourse around the practice of multifaceted urban planning and subsequently to the demand for a new type of public space in the city. The local citizen-led planning committee, Common Grounds, was created to invite all relevant local stakeholders to define their future needs in terms of space and its use. So instead of being sold off to the highest bidder at the end of the current lease, this very sensitive site in the middle of Berlin will strive to evolve into a coproduced multipurpose public space.

© dieLaube #GrowTheCommons #VerticalGreen

Changwon
Three Cities: Assemblage Urbanism
Jinseok Park
Changwon City

Changwon's exhibition is based on the consolidation of the three cities of Masan, Changwon, and Jinhae, which made New Changwon one of the largest cities in Korea. Within the homogeneous political-economic framework, three cities with completely different political foundations, economic organizations,

Die Laube in the City Garden. © dieLaube #GrowTheCommons #VerticalGreen

and social features have been transformed into a city with bland architecture and places, in the process gradually losing their rich architectural heritage and social contexts. Entitled *Assemblage Urbanism* in reference to the general theme of *Imminent Commons*, Changwon's presentation is an investigation of this architectural phenomenon, constructed in the different urban settings of three cities and emerging out of political-economic interventions. Since the consolidation, the three cities have been charged with new functions and meanings by this new assemblage, where their urban elements are constantly combined and overlaid to become new active elements. Thus, the character of New Changwon's architecture rises up to the surface. The nature of New Changwon's architecture is being formulated not only by arranging new spatial functions and urban meanings, but also by the constant participation and intervention of its citizens.

The exhibition juxtaposes two conditions of the phenomenon of the three cities: a historical trajectory of urban plot formation contrasts with the social and physical parameters defining the buildings that illustrate their relationship to the idea of locality. Through the questions of how New Changwon builds and represents itself through architecture, Changwon's presentation is able to discuss the *powers* generating local architecture and commons in these three cities. The *powers* create not only unique architectural forms and plots of mixed urban origins, but also societal structures and narratives. We have selected three research projects from each city in order to contrast the two conditions of the phenomenon and embed our manifesto within the urban settings that were triggered by top-

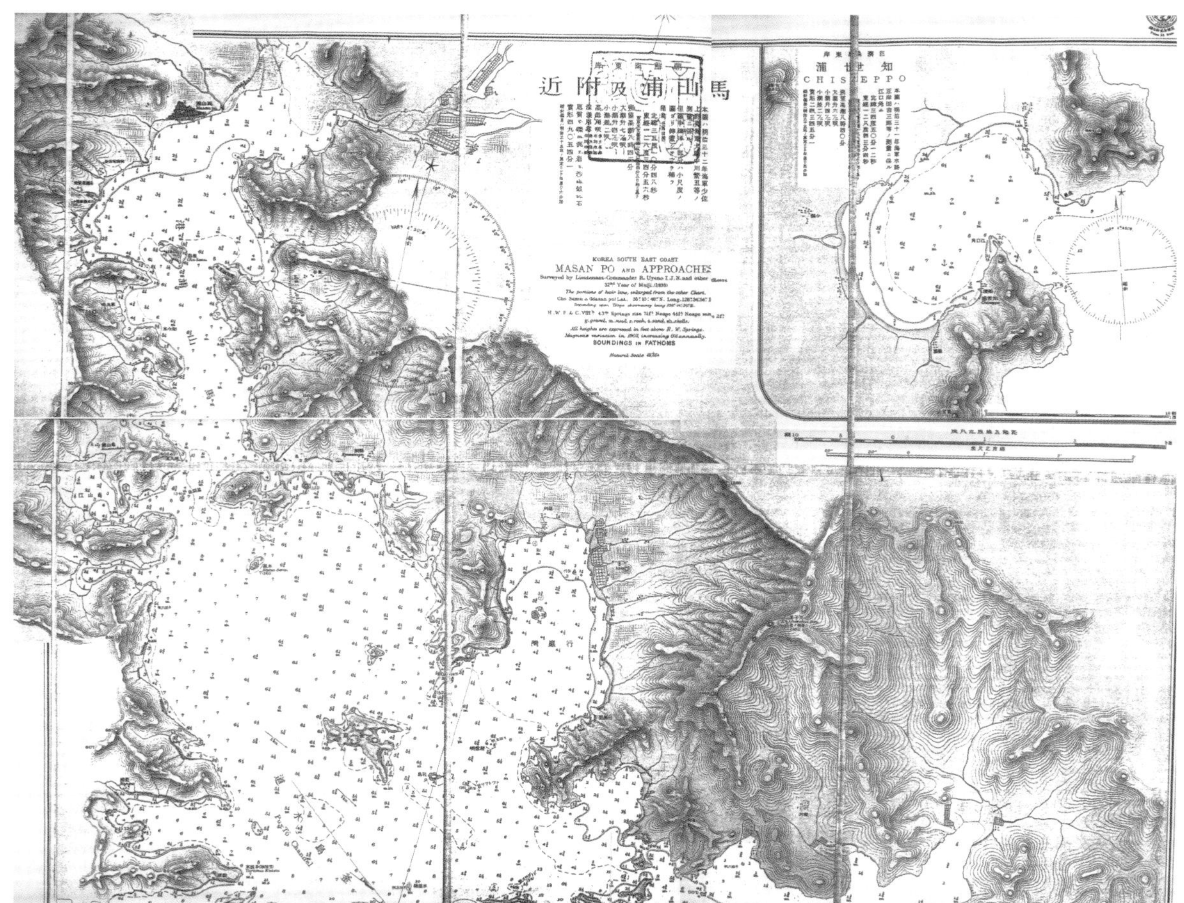

Masan Po and Approaches, 1899. Source: Hyungyoon Kim, *Masanyahwa.*

Japanese Street in Masan, 1920s. Source: Hyungyoon Kim, *Masanyahwa.*

down development. The first part of the exhibition comprises the various urban narratives that reveal the historical transformation and growth of the three cities in conjunction with their converging geography. Throughout the twentieth century, sudden changes in demographics, along with top-down development, produced hybrid architecture, especially in the residential sector. The combination of Japanese architecture, inevitable slum territories, and modern urban planning has cultivated an extraordinary urban landscape in the three cities. The second part of the exhibition involves territorial and architectural speculations of the tri-city combination. It illustrates the physical configurations and social narratives in the informal plots in Masan, as well as those in highly formal urban plots in Changwon and Jinhae. On the basis of our research, new architectural functions and roles for residential sectors in Masan, Changwon, and Jinhae are proposed as a suggested manifesto in order to invite the further participation and intervention of Changwon's citizens.

Chennai
At the Cross-Rivers: Reconnecting Chennai
Raghuram Avula
InKo Centre

Can a river and a city co-exist by sharing their resources and good will? With great effort, sincerity, and a unified vision, such a relationship can be created for the greater benefit of all.

Water is life, a natural gift that cleanses, quenches, moves, and fills us. Since ancient times, settlements have been created near rivers, lakes, and seas to harness this source of energy. Over time, some settlements have managed to evolve and sustain their connection with water. Such an evolution is visible in the vibrant city of Chennai. The vibrancy comes from the blend of its past, its growth, its resilience, and its humility. It is significant for being a state capital, a port, a transportation and industrial hub, as well as a cultural destination. The city leapt into global prominence during the IT boom, which created a burgeoning of architecture and infrastructure development.

Chennai has some unique bodies of water that have shone and faded over time, yet continue to engage the city with their potential to re-energize the urban environment. The city grew by having key roads connect various villages around the port. As the road networks spread, infrastructure and real estate developed along these corridors, while the bodies of water were sidelined and forgotten. Yet Chennai's connection with water reveals magnificent beaches, reservoirs and lakes, marshlands, canals, criss-crossing rivers, and mystical *eris* (irrigation tanks), creating a parallel and composite network that pours life into the city every day. As new settlements emerged, attracting people from all walks of life, the city became more cosmopolitan. The resulting architecture became layered, with multiple styles and interesting diversity; but with few exceptions, it showed very little relation to the bodies of water.

In current times, maintaining sufficient water for consumption, managing the sewage systems and responding to periodic water crises have been repeated challenges to this city, the fourth-largest in India, with a population of 8.5 million and growing.

Today we are at the crossroads, or should we say cross-rivers, as the resurgence in efforts to restore the rivers, replenish the reservoirs, reclaim the wetlands, and clean up the system opens up possibilities for creating the kind of new commons that all cities share, in order to establish a reconnection with water in a whole new way that is both new and linked to the past.

At the very beginning of this project, the need to understand Chennai's connection with water became paramount. It led us to explore the various typologies of bodies of water, the infrastructures for making potable water, the policies and the governing bodies that manage water resources, as well as sensitive issues that bring a whole new level of importance to this aspect of our lives that is second only to air. A city is not a singular entity, like a building that provides shelter, but a more complex evolution of space and structures over a great period of time; it takes its current form and aims to develop a sustainable platform for the growing population.

During our initial meetings with a group of architects and researchers, we discussed city life, the experiences and the growing density, stress levels, and so forth. Yet, there was a sense of hope when we looked into the past, as there were many clues that pointed to the possibility of a better urban paradigm. While some studied the historical evolution of city spaces, others were researching current urban expansions and the impact that they had. Overcrowding made the city lose some of its character. Poor policy implementation, too, diluted the vision of a grander city.

In the middle of all these discussions, the Cooum River emerged to show a charming character. We admired the way it meandered through the older part of the city and entered the sea oblivious to the unfair treatment meted out to it for the last few decades in the form of sewage and pollution. Earlier, the Cooum was a pristine river that had a legend of its own and defined the city as well. In fact, Chennai began near the mouth of the river, where it enters the Bay of Bengal. It was here that Fort St. George was built in the 1640s as a garrisoned factory by the British East India Company, marking the creation of this city. Though the Cooum is an ugly river now, filled with filth, reeking and lifeless, it flows with a certain energy and verve that reveals the inner light under all that darkness. With a restoration plan for the Cooum in progress, what were the possibilities?

Once again, we were at the cross-rivers. If this experiment of restoration succeeds, it will be a harbinger for a better architectural setting benefitting the whole city and its future. If it does not, will there be renewed interest in rethinking water policies and a greater will to keep existing bodies of water from disappearing completely?

We decided to focus on this historic river, which has witnessed many changing fates, and link the city into its context in a way that can generate a new architectural understanding.

Our collaborative studies of the city, the analysis of the riverfront, the graphic extractions of the various influencing factors, interviews and group discussions have helped us evolve an alternative way of looking at the urban fabric in direct relation to the water and the river. This has set the tone for a greater dialogue on water and the city.

The Chennai Pavilion examines some of the common strategies that are necessary to reclaim the city in a way that can enrich social experience and rebuild its lost character. Clues from the past, lessons from the present, and scenarios for the future are presented to build a new narrative for the city based on urban design methodologies.

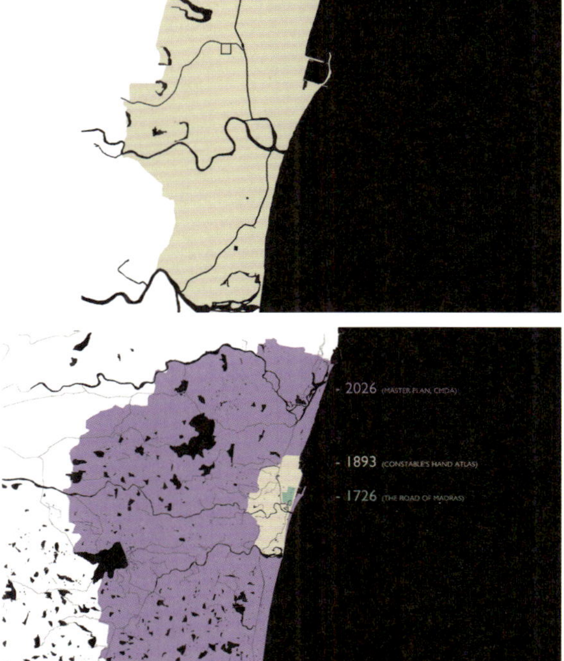

© Kumarappan Balagi

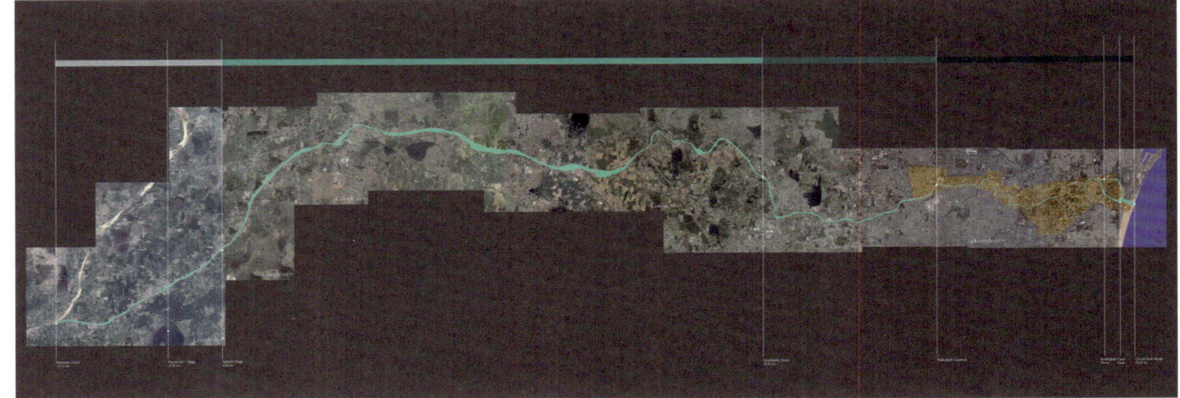

© Kumarappan Balagi. Maps courtesy of Google Earth

Because it is a testing time for the river as well as the people who connect with it, the exhibits visualize and analyze the interconnections between the river and the city at several transects, offering a better understanding of the relationship. Observations of the flood plains, the riparian corridor, and the response from the built environment have been compared and studied in order to present a greener, more sustainable scenario for the city in the future.

A historical analysis, which simultaneously compares the evolution of the city and the various bodies of water, throws light on the various factors that govern its growth and regulate its future course.

The architectural overlays with the proposed restoration of the river and future land use patterns allow us to explore the ideas of moving, sharing, and connecting more intuitively. The pavilion explores a larger urban context along the river for developing architectural connections that allow people to use the city more effectively through community participation and social interaction.

The meandering river also creates a new navigational path to access the heritage structures and cultural spaces that adorn the city, by using lighter modes of transportation, relieving the congestion of some of the denser areas.

Aligning the city with this river as well as other bodies of water using similar methodologies offers new opportunities for a well-connected architectural environment and great social benefit.

Though the river cuts through the city in its physical form, it also carves out a symbolic strand that can serve as an axis to invigorate the cultural, ecological, and socio-economic zones, restoring a lost value and eventually generating a stronger, more positive identity for the city.

Chinese Cities
Ghost Cities: Understanding Patterns in Chinese Urbanization
Civic Data Design Lab
MIT

After twenty years of exponential growth, vacant neighborhoods and cities are symbols of the slowing pace of the Chinese real estate market. These places—often referred to as "ghost cities"—were not abandoned; rather, no one ever moved in once they were built. The economic drivers behind this phenomenon are complex, but fundamental causes include a lack of jobs, schools, and city services as well as an oversupply of housing stock. China's overdevelopment and dependence on housing as an investment strategy made these areas more vulnerable to widespread economic slowdown.

Although little information existed about the locations or extent of these ghost cities, the Massachusetts Institute of Technology's Civic Data Design Lab developed a model to document them using data scraped from social media and websites—Dianping (Chinese Yelp), Amap (Chinese MapQuest), Fang

© Civic Data Design Lab, MIT: Sarah Williams, Zhekun Xiong

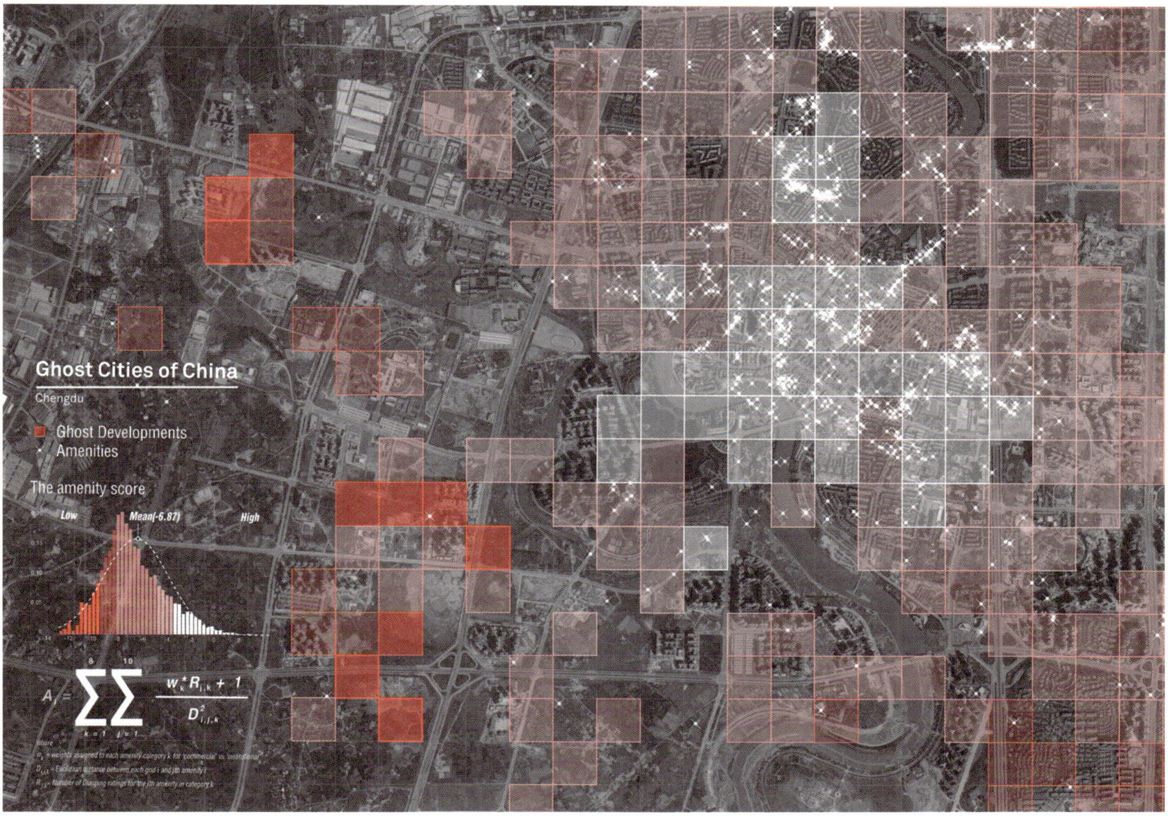

© Civic Data Design Lab, MIT: Sarah Williams, Wenfei Xu and Chaewon Ahn

(Chinese Zillow), and Baidu (Chinese Google Maps)—and by using openly accessible Application Programming Interfaces (APIs).

The result is one of the first maps to locate ghost cities, and it provides information critical for addressing strategies for planning and development. The data could help economists quantify the overleveraged Chinese real estate market and estimate its risks. The data could also allow local planners, developers, and citizens to make better investment decisions by confirming that these areas are indeed vacant.

To start, the model identified places without key amenities such as stores, restaurants, and schools, which suggested no one lived there. Using data scraped from social media sites in the cities of Chengdu and Shenyang, the model was tested using 300-by-300-meter grid cells marking residential locations. Each cell was given an amenity accessibility score based on distance and clustering of nearby amenities. Residential areas that had a cluster of low scores were marked as ghost cities. That designation was verified through site visits, drone photography, and interviews with local stakeholders.

Ghost Cities of China presents the results—one of the first maps of the ghost city phenomenon in China. Using interactive screens and dramatic drone imagery, the exhibition immerses visitors in these vacant cities, which were vulnerable because of overdevelopment as the Chinese economy slowed down.

The exhibition highlights the research project's unique process of combining quantitative data models with qualitative data obtained through ground-truthing. Interviews with local government officials, real estate developers, local academics, and planners are coupled with data visualizations of the model results and drone imagery.

Visitors entering the exhibition watch drone footage of ghost cities Shenyang, Tianjin, and Xudong, which were identified by the model. A video explains the data analysis process, including the novelty of scraping data from Chinese social media sites. Interviews with government officials, academics, and developers tell the full story of policy and macro factors that created ghost cities. An interactive map allows visitors to browse through the cities we modeled and learn more about the characteristics of the vacant real estate developments.

Dubai
Projected Futures for the Commons in Dubai

George Katodrytis
Mi Chang
Maryam Mudhaffar
Kevin Mitchell

In response to the theme of *Imminent Commons*, this exhibition on Dubai considers how the notion of the "commons" applies in a city that is characterized by extreme diversity and varying degrees of belonging. Dubai has long been an important node within a broader network of trade, and this has resulted in unique circumstances that present challenges as well as opportunities to urbanism.

Dubai is a city that has evolved through rapid transformation. It is unique among world cities in many ways, not least of which is in terms of population distribution: only approximately 10% of its inhabitants are citizens of the United Arab Emirates. As a point of comparison, the World Migration Report notes that Brussels has the next largest imbalance between expatriates and citizens, with citizens comprising 38% of the city's population.

In keeping with the Seoul Biennale of Architecture and Urbanism's focus on the future of the city in the face of radical social, ecolog-

Dubai spices souk (street market). © Photo by participating team of Reyan Hanafi, Noora Al Awar, Fatima Al Zaabi and Kh

Dubai map of proposals for the "commons" by 9 teams of 20 multiethnic designers representing a collective aspiration of the city.
GoogleEarth / Image © 2017 DigitalGlobe

ical, and technical transformation, the exhibition on Dubai presents a series of proposals that consider what can be "common" in a city that is defined by diversity. The exhibition, which comprises proposals by an emerging generation of architects and designers, critically examines the challenges and possibilities associated with expatriate existences in order to project an urban future.

EM/MENA
Connecting Cities: Commonalities and Challenges

Melina Nicolaides
The Future Earth MENA Regional Center
(FEMRC)

"What makes the desert beautiful is that somewhere it hides a well."
—Antoine de Saint-Exupery

The EM/MENA region refers to the geographical expanse that encompasses the Eastern Mediterranean, Middle East, and North Africa. This area not only possesses one of the fastest growing populations in the world, but also has been identified as the first region that will eventually remain waterless in the future due to largely man-made climate change. Home to a combined population of some 500 million people, it has been identified as a climate change "hot spot," as it represents a region already facing difficult conditions—and extreme predictions—for the future.

Today, this region is confronted with many interconnected challenges, such as increasingly over-exploited natural resources, rapid population growth, and spreading urbanization, and the multiple impacts of climate change. Commonalities and interactions between the increasing pressures on water supply, energy generation, and food security have already caused unprecedented challenges for cities and communities of the region. The difficulties faced by people within their daily lives, both in urban centers and in rural areas, are often remarkably similar. Climate change

The EM/MENA Region is characterized by strong environmental and climatic gradients, but with common bio-geographical characteristics. It has a high degree of urbanization. The region saw a 400% growth in urban structures during 1970 to 2010. It is expected that over the next 40 years there will be an additional 200% growth of larger cites.

Near-surface winds over the EM/MENA region which mobilize dust, mainly from the Sahara Desert, are transported across the region east and northwards covering Egypt, Crete, Cyprus, and parts of Greece and Turkey. Source: The Cyprus Institute.

and the effects of human intervention have also had an impact on environmental integrity and the health of regional ecosystems. From the wetlands of the Eastern Mediterranean to the Sahara Desert, the dangers of continued biodiversity loss and spreading desertification, often the result of degraded landscapes due to over-grazing or intensive farming, and the over-exploitation of water resources, have had devastating impacts on ecological balances.

Various locations across the EM/MENA region are also undergoing drastic political and societal transitions, armed conflict, and forced migration, which have pushed societal and en-vironmental systems to critical thresholds that can no longer buffer more external shocks, such as extreme drought or new waves of refugees. As a result of these developments, many communities of the region now face a combination of extraordinary challenges to the future welfare of their environments, livelihoods, human health, and even their cultures. The need for adaptation strategies that are both appropriate and regionally applicable is paramount in order to be able to assure the future availability of water, food, and energy to all peoples across this region.

The anticipated impacts of changing

weather patterns and climatic conditions are expected to have particularly strong manifestations in urban settings and to increase in severity over time; thus, climate change introduces exceptional demands on the cities of this region. This project intends to provide insights into current and future conditions by presenting an overview of the adaptive challenges of climate change in the urban context of the EM/MENA area. Each participating city will be represented by basic statistical and demographic data, which corresponds to these urban challenges. Additionally, comparative data from numerical climate models of the region such as measuring temperature and rainfall, plus air quality values, will help illustrate how the growing pressures of extreme conditions, such as hotter and drier summers, will be most intensely felt within urban centers.

The larger purpose of this regional initiative is to set in motion an effort to connect the adaptation strategies being developed by major regional institutions with solutions for common problems. As most cities face increased urbanization and population movements toward urban centers, climate change adaptation must now be considered a necessary part of every city's urban planning processes. This applies not only to impacts, but also to larger climate resilience strategies to reduce risk and vulnerability. City living conditions and human interaction with the built environment must be addressed. Factors that affect the realities of everyday life, such as enhanced urban warming and deteriorating air quality with resultant adverse health effects for city inhabitants, must be incorporated into effective mitigation and adaptation strategies for the projected extremes of the future.

The long-term objective of this ongoing EM/MENA project is to connect the knowledge of key regional institutions through an exchange not only between countries, but also with individuals and communities engaged in innovative methods and creative nature-based regenerative solutions "on the ground." The reality is that this region and our contemporary way of life, just like other areas of the world, has already passed its tipping point and is producing negative effects and unwanted alterations to our urban and natural environments. The merging of these two fields of knowledge, the mainstreaming of transformative adaptation into all sectors of society, may assist in the creation of better co-developed and integrated solutions for the future, so that we might be able to ensure resilience for the region's water sources, energy production and food security in the twenty-first century.

Nicosia
Climate Change Hot Spot: Future's Extremes
Melina Nicolaides
The Cyprus Institute

"Look at things from the end, and from their end to their beginning, because water goes and sand stays."
—Theoklis Kouyialis

The city of Nicosia is the political, economic and cultural capital of the Republic of Cyprus. This island, situated in the Levantine Sea, is projected to experience extreme climate warming similar to that expected in the entire Eastern Mediterranean, which has been designated as a climate change "hot spot" in the foreseeable future. After decades of industrialization, urban expansion and rapid population growth, the environmental challenges currently faced by the whole region will have increasingly adverse consequences for those living in the area's ever-growing cities. Anticipated phenomena—such as extreme weather events and deteriorating air quality—require that these cities incorporate more climate resilience strategies into their development plans, including policies for protecting human health. As the city of Nicosia already faces the effects of these concurrently emerging conditions, this interactive digital project envisions the lives of its residents in the future. Using the historical city center of Nicosia, contained within mid-sixteenth–century Venetian-era fortifications—built in the shape of a star with eleven bastions and three main gates— as a backdrop, an imagined environment of projected future conditions will portray the anticipated extreme living conditions of this evolving urban "hot spot."

For the contemporary urban environment

Nicosia inside and outside the Venetian walls. The city of Nicosia was contained within these walls until the first opening made in 1879 through one of its main gates. Following rapid urbanization and social change following Cypriot independence in 1960, the city spread into a continuously expanding built-up zone. Source: Yiannis Yiannelos, Troia Publishing SA, 2017.

Visualization within the historical city center, of the extreme dust event that took place on September 8, 2015 as seen in virtual reality using the Nicosia simulation model of The Cyprus Institute.

of Nicosia, the effects of a changing climate imply longer and more intense heat waves throughout the summer months, reduced rainfall, and a higher number of extreme weather events throughout the year—including few, but high-intensity rainstorms and subsequent flooding events, and extremely hot summer days and nights with maximum temperatures consistently exceeding 38 degrees Celsius. Moreover, Nicosia will see deteriorating air quality due to the trans-boundary effects of strong dust storms and pollutant influx from outside Cyprus—atmospherically transported desert sand from North Africa or the Arabian Peninsula. In combination with low air quality, these conditions will present serious health risks to the city's inhabitants. Comparable to other major cities in the region, the effects of climate change are expected to increase in severity over time; in the arid and semi-arid environments of the Mediterranean and MENA regions, these extended heat waves will have multiple consequences for those living in urban settings and will trigger significant side effects, including population movement, especially in the driest cites in close proximity to desert areas.

This interactive project presents possible extreme future scenarios regarding heat waves, dust and floods. Immersive visualizations of temperature peaks, rainfall extremes and flooding of urban Nicosia, as well as intense atmospheric events, will be presented in a virtual reality environment. In this dynamic setting, enacted within the walled city perimeters, simulations of walking between historic city structures and narrow streets will illustrate human conditions under these extreme circumstances. It will also envision how these environmental threats will affect city structures and the everyday activities of daily life. This includes the critical need for shade while moving about on foot, dust events that obstruct vision and cause respiratory difficulties and increased energy consumption for indoor cooling systems.

The primary objective of this presentation is to bring awareness and to emphasize the pressing need to prepare for and adapt to extreme living conditions in the urban spaces of the future. These projections illustrate how adaptation measures might have multiple effects, such as modifying human living, socio-economic circumstances and perhaps even transforming the character of the city itself. The project's immersive scenarios make it possible to visualize the implications of climate adversity within Nicosia and other similar cities of this region. Alongside this intention, the objective is also to serve members of the scientific disciplines in their efforts to design adaptive urban systems for Nicosia's development plans for both the population living in the historical city within the walls, and in the greater metropolitan area.

Throughout its long past, Nicosia has faced historical flooding events, evident in old city records and accounts, but also water scarcity and hot summers. Today, air quality limits in the urban context are frequently exceeded, even in winter months. As the projected impacts of climate change become better understood, the need for more adaptation measures—for example, more efficient stormwater management, measures against extreme urban warming, such as "cool pavements" or additional shading, and the need for more green spaces—becomes more apparent. The hope is that any new approaches and responses for climate change adaptation for Nicosia may also provide valuable strategies for other urban centers and "hot spot" cities in the EM/MENA region, and contribute to safeguarding the well-being of the people throughout the region against future extremes—as populations, urbanization, and development continue to increase in the years to come.

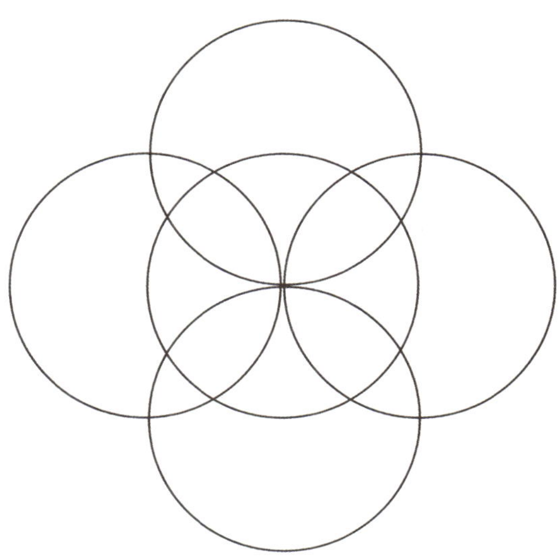

Diagram of Solon's Water Law, which corresponds to five neighboring Athenian wells where ideal distances between each one is 740 meters.

Athens
From Antiquity to Tomorrow: The People's Water Project

Melina Nicolaides
EYDAP

"Water, the beginning of all things [*Nero, arxi ton panton*]."
—Thales of Miletus, c. 600BCE

Since the time of its birth, the city of Athens has lived with the notion that the perennial shortage of water faced by its inhabitants is rooted in a mythical contest between Olympian gods Poseidon and Athena. Hence, it was from that time onward that this city had to develop basic water collection and distribution systems for the freshwater needs of the people. Historic projects were constructed to supply drinking water, and to provide high living standards and hygiene to the inhabitants of Attica. The ancient Athenians not only engineered works to provide sufficient quantities of water, but also took measures to preserve water quality and promote rational usage of the scarce resource. With projects such as aqueducts, fountains, wells, reservoirs, and distribution networks, they ensured that the inhabitants of Attica would always have a constant supply, despite the permanent threat of water shortage.

With the passing of time and the progress of technology into the modern era, the role both of provider and of "water-keeper" for the contemporary city passed into the hands of the Athens public water authority. Today, EYDAP—the largest water and wastewater management company in Greece—undertakes the responsibility for supply, distribution, quality control, sewerage and water treatment plants, irrigation, and infrastructure maintenance. With these responsibilities, it sustains and upholds the duty first embodied in the ancient constitutional "water law" enacted by Athenian statesman Solon in the year 530 BCE. This earliest recorded regulation referring to water usage, ensured that any Athenian citizen who had no groundwater source of his own was afforded the right to take water from a neighbor's well. At present, the water of Athens is among the highest quality water in all of Europe, and potable water reaches the nearly six million residents of the area through an extensive distribution network of over 9,500 kilometers. EYDAP safeguards the basic human right to clean water and sanitation, as well as the ecological protection of this resource in the natural environment of Greece.

The EYDAP water project was designed as a visually descriptive water chronology;

Construction of underground water tunnel that would transport water from the Marathon Reservoir to the city of Athens for the first time. Boyiati Tunnel 1928. Source: Historical Archive EYDAP.

it presents a historical overview of the water supply and management of this ancient city and the district of Attica. Through the framework of an interactive digital map, it is possible to reveal images that correspond to historical water sites and contemporary hydrological networks. In this way, it creates the experience of being able to transition across different eras and locations, creating links between people of different communities, neighborhoods, and ancestries. The connective possibilities generated by this network grid make possible new symbolic narratives between all the people who have at one time in history accessed the waters of Attica.

The imagery of this project, assembled from the archives of EYDAP, reveals important milestones in the story of Athenian water. Such instances include ancient Athenians using the Hadrian Aqueduct system, or the arrival of refugees and immigrants from Asia Minor in 1922, a seminal moment in the water history of Athens, in which a sudden increase in population required supplementary sources for the city's water supply—a task accomplished with the building of the celebrated Marathon Dam. Contemporary water network images might correspond to visiting tourists at a drinking fountain within the ancient historic marketplace, or to the city's peripheral Aspropirgos source, which provides water to today's transient population of Syrian refugees.

As the water history of Attica has always been associated with the quality of life, the progress, and the expansion of this city, it can be said that her citizens, and the people who to this day pass through Athens, have truly always been connected—physically, socially, culturally—by this one commons. Likewise, as connectivity is essential to communication and mutual understanding in the twenty-first century, interaction with this project's network will enable, firstly, an understanding of the relationship different people have had with Athenian water over the centuries. Moreover, it will also affirm the principle that water is a resource that belongs to all people. This presentation proposes that, within a society, this common resource should be an example both of city-to-citizen reciprocity, and of human interdependency—following the water ethics of ancient Athens. Any endangerment of this communal heritage or reversal of this prescript would threaten the very identity of this city, its historical past, and its connection to its future self.

Alexandria
After Past and Present:
Determining the Future

Melina Nicolaides
Bibliotheca Alexandrina

"Alexandria does not leave, but leaves the world her eternal Alexandrianism."
—Dr. Mohammed Awad

The legendary metropolis and enduring city of Alexandria was founded in 331 BCE alongside the waters of the Mediterranean Sea by Alexander the Great. It was designed by his architect and urban planner, Dinocratis, to be the capital of Egypt and of the ancient world. Today, as Egypt's second-largest urban center, with a population of six million people, it is a major industrial hub, with a seaport that handles four-fifths of the country's national trade. Over the city's two millennia of urban evolution, this historically multicultural center of knowledge and exchange has cycled through stages of rebirth and collapse and has experienced an untold number of existential and physical transformations. This project juxtaposes the city's past, present, and possible future existences. It will serve to illustrate that the undetermined outcome of current urban challenges and rapidly changing environmental conditions will ultimately define the future identity of this city. In this present-day era of vulnerability, priority must be given to envisioning a new model of Alexandrine urbanism for the years to come.

In the city's more recent past, Alexandria experienced an urban revival, beginning in the early nineteenth century. At that time, the city developed into a model of intercultural

View of the "corniche" road showing the proximity of the sea waves to the city, and its vulnerability to the coastal implications of' climate change.

Seafront of Alexandria, facing the Eastern Harbor with its 15th century Fortress of Qaitbey, built on the site of the legendary Pharos - Alexandria's ancient lighthouse - one of the seven wonders of the ancient world. Visible is the West Harbor which handles most of Egypt's commercial shipping and foreign trade. Source: AlexMED, Bibliotheca Alexandrina.

Downtown neighborhood in Alexandria during the extreme rainfall event of October 2015. Source: Center for Sustainable Development Studies, Bibliotheca Alexandrina.

People walking along the wall of the "corniche" road, submerged by the floods of the extreme rainfall event of October 2015. Source: Center for Sustainable Development Studies, Bibliotheca Alexandrina.

exchange, pluralism, and tolerance, and it had a reputation for bustling cosmopolitanism. The onset of the twentieth century, however, represented a turning point characterized by unprecedented urban sprawl. This resulted

in a combination of human and architectural ataxia—literally, the loss of control over bodily movements—an urban disorder that continues today. An ongoing interplay of demolition and development brought on the contemporaneous spread of concrete buildings and the ruin of much of the city's distinctive architectural heritage. Modified human activity, occupational and population shifts, including refugee and displaced rural communities, brought compulsory alterations to urban settlements in order to meet the housing demands of the city. Waves of construction due to ongoing shifts in the socio-economic identity of the city and its residents continue to force unplanned physical changes on the city's structure and damage the city's urban character.

Today, the city of Alexandria faces challenges resulting not only from the human influence of this hasty and unsystematic expansion, but also from the increasing environmental threats of climate change. Always strongly linked with the sea, contemporary Alexandria is suffering the consequences of its distinctive coastal location. As an "exposed zone," it is considered a living example of the physical impacts of climate change and extreme weather events. These include extreme rainstorms and flooding, rising sea levels, and the effects of saline intrusion into its coastal aquifers—issues also faced by other urban centers situated along the Mediterranean.

Within this current urban reality, these parallel challenges affect both people and places in Alexandria. The city's streets, which are increasingly seawater-flooded following high-intensity storms, affect work and living spaces, and endanger historic monuments and the archeological sites of Alexandrine cultural heritage. Just as rising seas and powerful wave surges erode waterfront beach areas and the seaside "corniche" road cut into the cliffs—both traditionally part of the daily lives of Alexandria's residents—the barrier walls around the historical Eastern Harbor are also experiencing the physical repercussions of these environmental forces. These combined factors have distressed Alexandria's already crumbling infrastructure, exposing the city's urban flaws and its vulnerable coastline.

As an insight into the city's future, this

project will look at strategies for both adaptation and transformation, specifically through a campaign and design competition to promote a preservation project for the Eastern Harbor. This site represents a principal feature of the city's founding design, which not only symbolizes the different historical phases in the development of the city, but also remains the most important spot identified with Alexandria's waterfront. A series of proposed megadevelopment projects fostered under the auspices of the Bibliotheca Alexandrina—in its historically influential role and active engagement with the progressive advancement of the city—put forward a new urban vision for an Alexandria of the twenty-first century.

Determining the future of Alexandria will require an approach that integrates core solutions to its current challenges of urban adaptation and coastal management, while also preserving the city's historical and architectural legacy. The forthcoming Alexandria must evaluate the scale of its present vulnerability and transform its dire economic, environmental, and technological obstacles. However, for this "eternal city" to ensure a bright future that will be on par with its illustrious past, it must formulate creative and human-centered responses that go beyond city planning—which might initiate the birth of a new urban Alexandrianism for its next generation of citizens.

Gwangju
Cultural Landscape of the City: Gwangju Folly
Hong-guen Park
Gwangju Biennale

In architecture, a "folly" is a building without a function; it is a building that is constructed primarily for decoration. However, in the case of *Gwangju Folly*, a folly is a structure that intervenes in public space and contributes to urban renewal. *Gwangju Folly* is a project that was initiated in 2011 by architects Seung H-Sang and Ai Weiwei, who came together as artistic directors of the Gwangju Design Biennale. Inaugurated as part of that biennale, the project marks its third iteration in 2017 as it continues to introduce a series of new follies

Leif Hogfeldt Hansen, *Spectrum*, 2016. © gwangjufolly.org

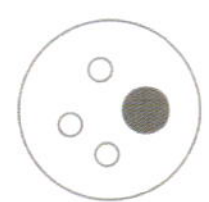    

in Gwangju, a city deeply interwoven into narratives of the modern history of Korea.

Placed within the heart of the old urban centers of Gwangju, areas that have been experiencing severe decline due to the rapid expansion of the city into new urban centers, the Gwangju follies have generated waves of strong cultural energy. It is anticipated that the project will serve as a starting point for the old downtown's urban renewal. In this context, rather than existing and functioning as individual and separate entities, the Gwangju follies are increasingly becoming a collective unit; they form a pattern as a collective and are expected to exert influence as such.

Managed by the Gwangju Biennale Foundation, the first set of follies traced the ancient town wall of Gwangju and restored historical footprints into everyday modern urban life. The project's next set of follies then intervened in the spaces of the city's modern and contemporary history where it explored the potentialities of the city's sociopolitical consciousness. This year, *Gwangju Folly III* penetrates into everyday urban spaces and carries out various cultural and artistic experiments. It presents new possibilities for the project; providing novel experiences, a renewal of declining urban areas, and job opportunities for young people. In a work entitled *Spectrum*, a moveable "mini folly," Leif Hogfeldt Hansen shows a history of the project through a series of panel installations and video work. The work shows how *Gwangju Folly* started as a public art project, the locations of the follies, the construction process, the potential for the project's growth, and future tasks and expectations. In particular, the work explains the diverse viewpoints of *Gwangju Folly III*, emphasizing the project's relationship with the local community. It shows the way the follies are perceived by the local population and the role that the follies play in everyday life. The video shows the current images of the follies installed at various sites and assesses their role and function.

Hong Kong / Shenzhen
By-City / By-Product
Peter W. Ferretto
Doreen Heng Liu

Contemporary cities never start nor end; rather, they continuously adapt, mitigate, and mutate to remain relevant, expanding and contracting to survive. Several hundred million more people are expected to move to cities in East Asia over the next twenty years as economies shift from agriculture and manufacturing to services. When China's Pearl River Delta has overtaken Tokyo to become the world's largest urban area in both size and population, Hong Kong (HK) and Shenzhen (SZ) are in a strategic position, both geographically and politically, to examine the role of what our cities are, rather than what they might become.

Inspired by observations of real urban settings, *By-City / By-Product* examines the contemporary city as a series of conditions, no longer under the control of architects, urbanists, or planners, but governed by multiple coexisting agents. Hong Kong and Shenzhen are analyzed not through abstract postula-

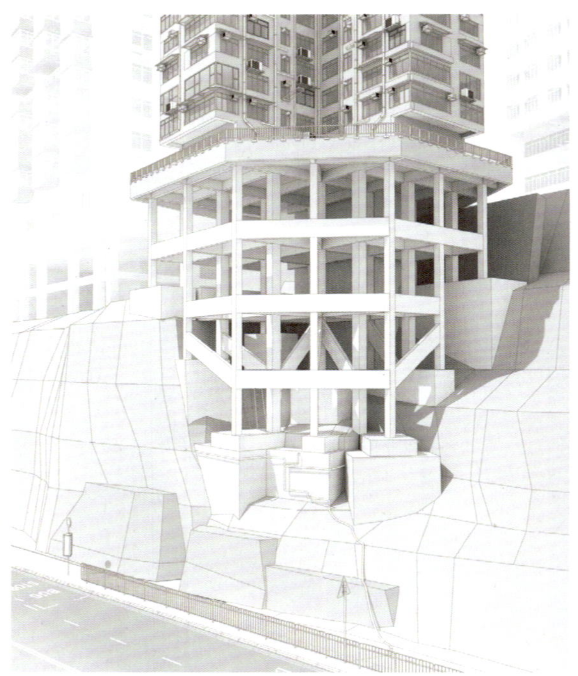

Condition / Engineered Landscape. © Sungyeol Choi / Peter W. Ferretto

tions based on preconceived models, but by focusing on the present reality of the city, the actual urban everyday that stares at us in the face, the urban presence of the here and now.

Both cities share a complex, interconnected, yet detached existence, yet they remain connected in their engineered nature, where their physical territory is constantly adapted to mitigate the changing conditions. Looking at these two cities from two different perspectives—micro inhabitation (HK) and macro temporality (SZ)—generates a discussion about cultural identity, that is, the way of life of the city in an age of globalization. The two fragments constructed aim to reveal an "urban dialect" unique to HK and SZ, one that avoids the stereotypical and preconceived analysis we so often fall prey to.

"By-product" here refers to the leftover city that we inhabit: the interstitial, hidden, and marginal. By physically recreating one of these HK conditions in Seoul, and juxtaposing it with time fragments from South Korea, visitors are forced to ask questions, and through these questions engage with the content of the exhibition, which reveals different facets of these two cities.

Hong Kong Conditions

At the core of what defines an urban condition is the notion of how we inhabit a space. These two words—"inhabit" and "space"—are the essence behind adapting urban conditions, that is, how physical spaces mutate to accommodate human existence, participation, and engagement. Conditions do not follow predetermined or preconceived ideals of spatial inhabitation; rather, they reflect a constantly adapting space, a space that is arranged in association with time. The urban conditions we are confronted with in Hong Kong are based on the unique ground reality of the city; a landscape that constantly transforms, reliant on temporary existence. This kinetic urban reality, common to many Asian cities, generates a temporal background of overlaying circumstances, each associated with a unique by-product: planning codes, building regulations, government covenants, etc. To this effect urban conditions are relative entities, dependent on specific spatial relationships, which at first sight might not be evident, but only appear the more you digest the condition via observation, mapping, and drawing. These urban relationships, given Hong Kong's density, generate a general condition of intensity reliant on multiple networks of activity.

Shenzhen—Juxtaposition of Time

Thanks to its inherent geopolitical location in the Pearl River Delta and the immediate adjacency of Hong Kong, Shenzhen is actually an exemplar of the significant transformation that has taken place in China. In just over three decades, Shenzhen has experienced explosive growth—from a small frontier town

Shennan Road, Shenzhen. © photo by Bai Xiao-Ci

with a population of 30,000 to a metropolis of 200 million residents—a process that might have taken hundreds of years in the industrial revolution of Western countries. Driven by the trinity of the sweeping globalization process, the powerful top-down practices of the Chinese government, and the egoic boost of becoming "top-of-the-town," and using the methods of Western modern planning, Shenzhen has rapidly and miraculously developed an appearance that is commonly seen in Western cities and has become representative of the high efficiency city, where capital is admired above all else. In 2016, Shenzhen was number four in GDP in the country; it is now aimed at number one, and will probably get there in two years' time. Obviously, without the presence of Hong Kong, Shenzhen would not have been born in the first place. The exhibition is about time and perception of time in Shenzhen, a full exploration of Shenzhen as "by-city/by-product" in relation to Hong Kong. Now, as a strong competitor and collaborator, Shenzhen is pursuing its own destiny. The exhibition also looks into the future of Shenzhen as the conclusion of this pursuit.

Jakarta
Micro Practice and Macro Perspective for Building Resilience in an Urban *Kampung*
Megacity Design Lab

Since 2011, one *kampung* (slum) in Cikini, Central Jakarta, has become a living laboratory for Universitas Indonesia, Chiba University, and the University of Tokyo. The goal is to provide students with the opportunity to integrate design, participatory work with the community, and the prevailing universal view that architecture is a tool to empower the community. Megacity Design Lab was established as a learning platform for students to work with communities, and to explore and find design methods by relying on local knowledge while preserving the local environment.

Kampung Cikini Kramat, or Cikini Ampiun, is one of the most densely populated urban kampungs in Jakarta. Located in the center of the city, this four-hectare kampung is accessible from various nodes around the area.

Kampung Cikini is inhabited by 3,200 people from lower-middle-class backgrounds. With poor environmental and health conditions, residents of Kampung Cikini have to face multidimensional problems in their daily lives. The big question that challenges us is, How can we, in our capacity and creativity, contribute solutions to this complex and multidimensional problem?

We try to look towards architectural education as one way to answer this challenge. With the full consciousness that conventional city planning as adopted from the West is not sufficient to respond to changing issues in big cities in the Global South, we would like to offer the kampung as a vanguard of architecture and urban design in addressing global issues related to poverty and climate change. We realize that the outdated paradigm of looking at the kampung needs to change; from understanding the kampung as "the source of the problem" to "a solution and a reservoir of learning material." As a community, the kampung is not just a complementary object, but a partner to enrich knowledge in architecture and urban design. Our approach to completing the project in Kampung Cikini could be analogous to a "sandwich" of top-down and bottom-up approaches, with special emphasis on strengthening local values and confirming the members of the community as the main actors.

The six years of the Cikini Project's experiences have provided a first-hand view of kampung problems and solutions in all their complexity and possibility. Our projects on common places studied the activities of the assembly and collective action. We want to intensify the collective consciousness between the communities through promoting alternative models of common places and improving the current unsustainable model.

In dealing with kampung commons, we opened the possibility of moving beyond the old "formal-informal" debate and called for a bridging of formal-informal. We considered that the peculiarity of the character of informal settlements is that the common spaces are not intentionally designed, as they exclusively are in modern and formal urban design. The "commonness" of this space has been

Cikini, Central Jakarta © Evawani Ellisa

formed through the practices and uses of people, which can be chaotic, but in fact there is some order underlying the chaotic-looking space. Furthermore, commons in the kampung are inclusive of inhabitants but are excluded from the formal real estate market. The resilience of urban kampung commons demonstrates the possibility for a symbiosis of the market economy and urban commons.

In the exhibition, we will introduce Kampung Cikini and show how to work effectively to find sustainable solutions through designing commons, which combine micro practices with macro and long-term intervention practices. The exhibition will show how residents of Kampung Cikini creatively try to negotiate their everyday activities in a densely populated area. It is presented as an integrated part of our projects on common places, which serve the activities of assembly and collective action. Through our experiences we want to show that the design of common ground at Kampung Cikini is a platform toward alternative ways of designing the commons.

The increasing concern for limited resources, as well as a rapidly growing population, forces us to re-evaluate our ways of living. Our current practices in Megacity Design Lab since 2011, as a laboratory for international collaboration between Japan and Indonesia, address this issue by putting architectural and urban design practices within the community of Kampung Cikini. In this exhibition, we attempt to illustrate a different perspective: seeing densely populated areas as an alternative way of living as well as celebrating the urban commons that are revealed within communities. This exhibition, thereby, offers us a huge opportunity to show the emerging discourse from our practices to a wider audience.

Jeju
Dolchanggo: Between Home and Nomadism, Jeju Rurbanism

Seongcheon Ko
Jeju Special Self-Governing Province & KIRA
Jeju Chapter of Korea Institute of
Registered Architects

The volcanic island of Jeju lies off the southern coast of the Korean Peninsula. The island is formed of the volcanic rock basalt, making farming and the lives of the Jeju people difficult. When development on the island began in the 1960s, income for local residents began to improve through tourism and citrus farming; people's lives also began to improve. Tourism on the island has been particularly successful. Presently, tourists from all over the world, attracted by its natural beauty, come to Jeju. Add to this background the "back to the country" or "back to home" social trend within Korea, and you have a sizable population moving to Jeju Island. Foreign investment has increased dramatically, and that money is behind many of the large-scale resort developments. In the past five to six years, drastic changes have been taking place on Jeju.

"Rurbanism" is a new concept that explores the ways in which traditional rural villages and urbanism relate to each other in ways that can be complementary. It is a neologism that came to the fore at the dead end of mega-urbanization. It is a concept that is perhaps not too far removed from the idea of building *do-nong* (urban-rural) relationships, which has gained traction in Korea for some time. Rurbanism is now urgently needed in Jeju. Using the concept of rurbanism, the problems on the island can be solved through a tripartite framework, connecting the elements of the urban, the pastoral, and the neighborhood. Moreover, diversity must be

© Seongcheon Ko

encouraged in both large and small developments. They must be encouraged in order to protect the diversity of Jeju while at the same time satisfying newer desires. Jeju is at a crossroads where it must protect its identity.

The exhibition *Dolchanggo* illustrates the diverse changes currently taking place in Jeju: the term "Jeju phenomenon" refers to the recent sea-change rapidly taking place on the island. The transformation of the *dolchanggo*, a commonly found stone warehouse in the inland areas of the island, is a good example of this phenomenon.

The *dolchanggo*, typically built of local basalt, is a vernacular form of Jeju architecture. In the past, it represented citrus farming or a way of life that was attached to the land; today it signifies nomadism. It is in this regard that the *dolchanggo* gives us a portrait of the recent Jeju phenomenon. The *dolchanggo* is the intersection where the old and new settlers of Jeju meet; it is where new Jeju communities are being built; and it is where the urban and the rural create synergy. It is the rurbanism of today and a phenomenon unique to Jeju.

On the exhibition table, there are twenty or so small works of photography. The photographs, laid out in a way that tells a story, show natural and cultural elements of Jeju; they show structures, buildings, and the restoration process and preservation of a *dolchanggo*. An architectural model of an actual renovated *dolchanggo* is also on display. There are two projection screens; one, focused on settlement, shows the nature and culture of Jeju; another, focused on nomadism, shows various examples of the renovation of a *dolchanggo*.

Artist's Note

Jeju is a volcanic island. Lava erupted over a period of tens of thousands of years, hardened in the open air, and became basalt, a porous stone. Basalt is what gives Jeju its color and its scenery. Jeju is also the wind island; in the summer, it sits in the pathway of typhoons that come up from the South Pacific; in the winter, the northwestern continental winds rage across the island. It is not an ideal land for settlement. But the local residents were wise and resourceful, and they used the

© Seongcheon Ko

stone available in abundance everywhere on the island. From cradle to grave, every step and every aspect of the lives of the local residents are connected to stones; their very life, culture, and history are laminated on stones.

The current work is an attempt to reveal the Jeju phenomenon, that is, the recent phenomenon of changing patterns of life on Jeju Island from settlement to nomadism. In so doing, I trace the natural, cultural, and historical background of the lives of the local residents, starting with the origin of the stones on Jeju. The *dolchanggo* is an excellent visual aid for discussing this topic. In the past a *dolchanggo* symbolized the traditional agricultural life of Jeju. As "outside" people started coming onto the island to live, it has now gained new life from the nomadism of the contemporary population. These "nomads" who come to Jeju find value in the "aesthetics of originality," which they find in the *dolchanggo*. They then return the aesthetics they find into the sphere of everyday life.

As mentioned, I call such changes on the island the Jeju phenomenon; it represents the new, contemporary locality of Jeju. What we are doing in the exhibition is deconstructing the time that is laminated on the stones of Jeju; we do this through images that depict the beginning-settlement-nomadism connection. We begin the navigation in search of Jeju's placement in the sea of time that is the *dolchanggo*.

Johannesburg
Shifting Borders and Building Bridges
Gauteng City-Region Observatory

Borders are both material and unseen, constructed and imaginary, fixed and fluid. In recent years we have seen the continued relevance of international borders and how these affect the lives of people in different places. While political borders remain as pertinent as ever, this exhibition examines other kinds of "urban borders" in the context of the Gauteng City-Region(GCR).

Cities in South Africa are infamous for their divided and unequal geographies, a legacy of the colonial and apartheid planning policies. Despite significant efforts to integrate the GCR, apartheid's visible and invisible borders and barriers remain both in the material landscape and in the economic and social fabric. Although the history of apartheid is particular to South Africa, the inequality that the city-region faces resonates across many parts of the world.

This exhibition explores the making, shifting, and bridging of urban borders through four perspectives. The "Spatial" story map relays how—even though the political borders of provinces and "homeland" states were abolished with the end of apartheid and the first democratic elections in 1994—spatial segregation remains and recurs, in spite of the fact that other shifts have occurred in the last twenty years.

The "Social" story map illustrates how racist apartheid laws have re-emerged as social barriers, which can manifest in the urban landscape in such physical forms as gated communities.

The "Resource" story map shows how the broader context of the landscape and natural resources worked as a barrier shaping the history of development in the city-region, as well as how it will shape its future.

The "Institutional" story map explores how both government and academia are navigating these complexities while also encountering institutional and knowledge borders.

The Gauteng City-Region is South Africa's economic heartland and includes the cities of Johannesburg and Pretoria. It holds thirteen million people and generates a third of the South African GDP on 1.5% of its land area.

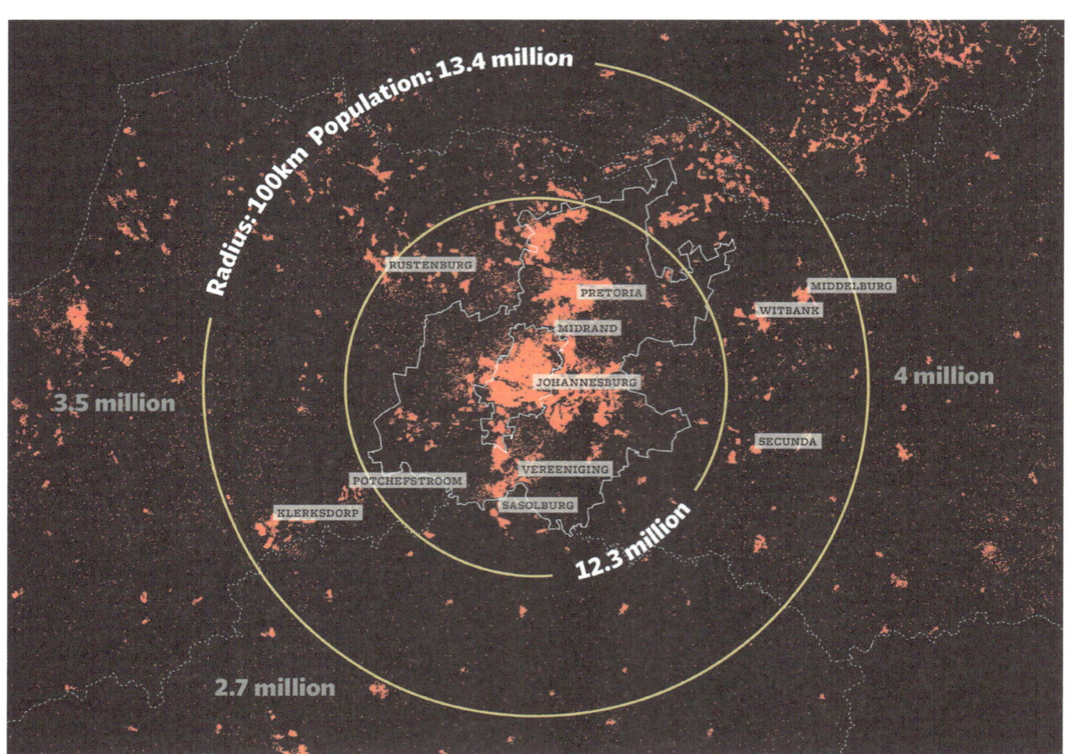

Map of the population density of the Gauteng City-Region. The map shows how the city-region extends beyond the provincial boundary of Gauteng. © Gauteng City-Region Observatory

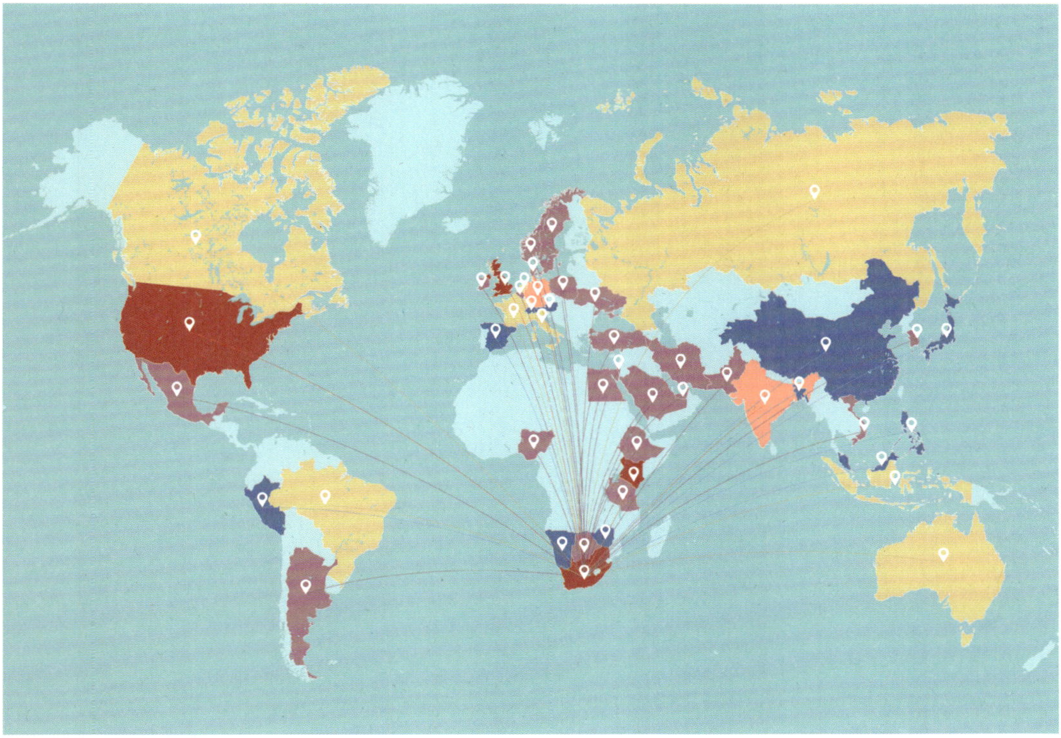

Map of global visitors to the Gauteng City-Region Observatory website. The map shows how information that is produced by the GCRO is accessed around the world. © Gauteng City-Region Observatory

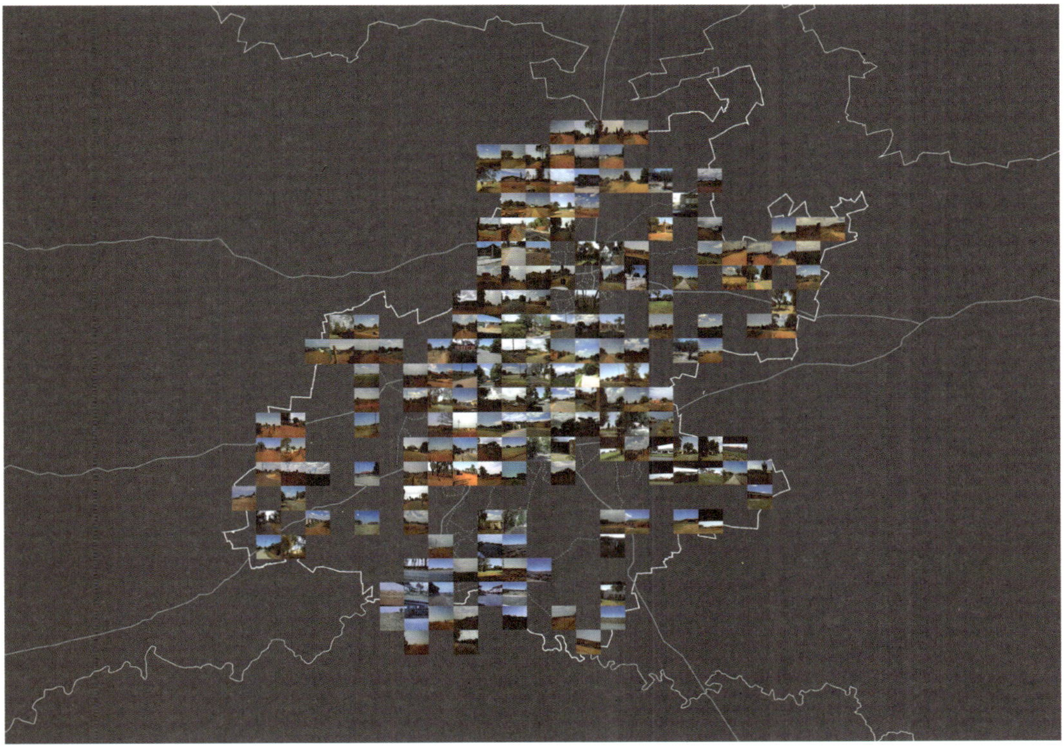

Map of the streets of the Gauteng City-Region. Echoing the production of aerial photos, the map constructs a composite image of Gauteng using geotagged photos of its streets. © Gauteng City-Region Observatory

Map of the sampling points for the GCRO Quality of Life Survey. Starting in 2009 the GCRO has run a biennial Quality of Life survey with responses from some 30,000 respondents in the province. © Gauteng City-Region Observatory

The Gauteng City-Region Observatory (GCRO) builds the data and analysis to help inform development in this region.

London

London Made

We Made That

Greater London Authority

London is well established as a productive city. Making and manufacturing can be found in many different parts of the capital, reflecting a wide range of sectors, from beer to bicycles and fashion to furniture.[1] Combined with logistics and other light industrial urban services, these play a vital role in London's economy, delivering the goods so essential for the capital to thrive. The city is home to a diverse range of workspaces, from converted warehouses to newly built industrial spaces and small-scale design and artist studios.[2] These support and sustain a huge array of industrial, urban service, and making activities. While there is much to celebrate, London is losing space for production and industry. The need to house a growing population within a constrained city region, and the resulting loss of industrial land, is reducing the city's capacity as a place of production. In the context of London's now well-documented loss of designated industrial land[3] manufacturers, food processers, urban logistics, and local service businesses are facing uncertainty about how they fit into London's future. It is more important than ever to defend London's industrial places and spaces. There is a need to think more imaginatively about what these sites can accommodate and how they might be adapted to keep existing and additional productive uses on site. Industrial sites are too often dismissed as "underused" parts of the city;

1. As illustrated by industrial audits in Park Royal, Upper Lea Valley, Old Kent Road, Charlton Riverside, Loughborough Junction, Royal Docks and the London Legacy Development Corporation area.

2. As detailed in "New London Architecture's WRK/LDN Insight Study."
3. "London Industrial Land Supply and Economy Study," 2015. AECOM, Cushman & Wakefield & We Made That, 2015.

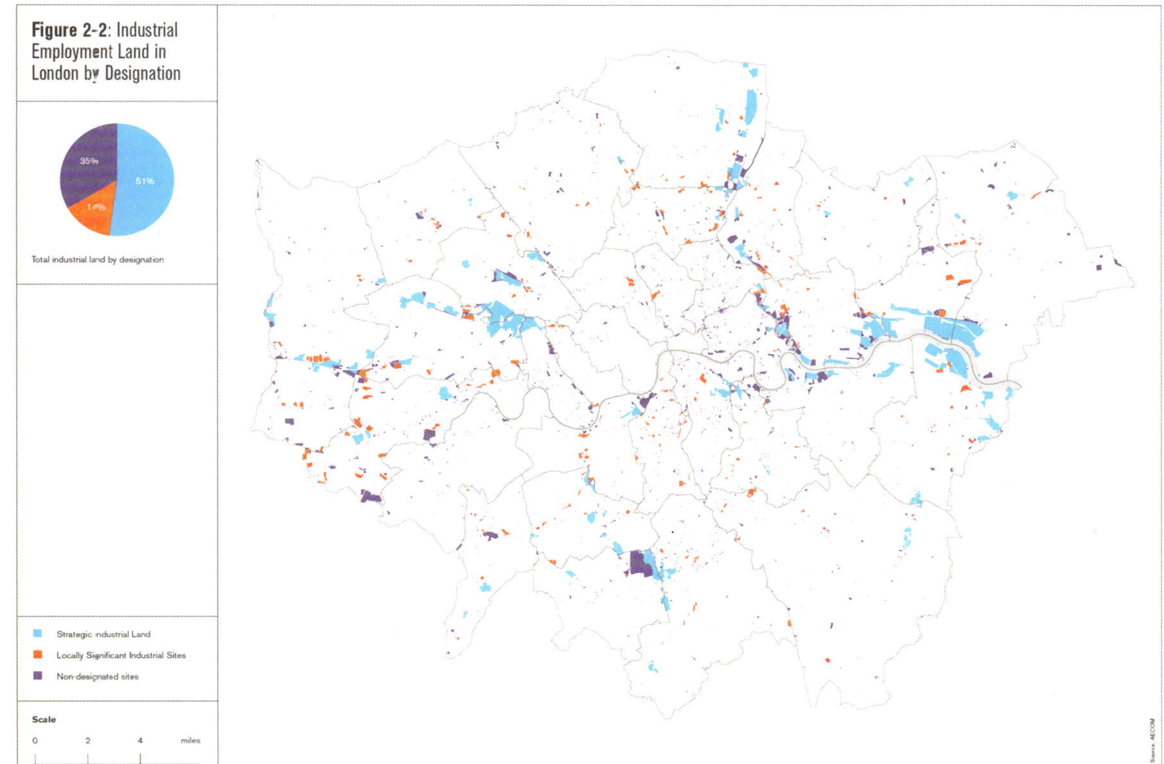

London's industrial land as of 2015. Since 2001, 1,305ha of industrial land has been released to non-industrial uses.
"London Industrial Land Supply and Economy Study," 2015. AECOM, Cushman & Wakefield & We Made That for Greater London Authority.

they take up a lot of space and can appear as hostile or neglected environments. Recent years of uncertainty have contributed further to this condition, but spaces for industry are undoubtedly more vital, fruitful, and colorful than the "brownfield" label that is often conveniently applied to them in anticipation of redevelopment.

London needs innovative ways to deliver more mixed, intensified, productive spaces. The Mayor of London, urban practitioners, local authorities, and industrial landowners are championing industrial intensification[4] key priority of the next London Plan. These ambitions should be quickly embraced and widely adopted in order to keep London a proudly productive city.

London Made, a film commissioned specially for the Seoul Biennale of Architecture and Urbanism, celebrates the people, processes, and places that make London a productive city.

The exhibition looks behind the stage to explore the "back of house" supply chains of the Barbican, one of London's most distinctive cultural venues. *London Made* follows a series of chains that lead out of the Barbican to uncover production activities and networks of supply that support and sustain the venue.

This exploration spans Greater London, uncovering layers of supply, from raw materials to final-stage installation and display. As well as cultural production processes such as set design, costume production, and audio-visual services, the chains featured in the film illustrate wider industrial activities, such as urban logistics, high-tech manufacturing, and food and drink production, which are crucial to keep the city thriving.

At the same time, this work looks beyond the current landscape to the policies, places, and pressures that shape how London works

4. As demonstrated in the Mayor of London's 2016 Industrial Intensification Primer, SEGRO's "Keep London Working" research, and case studies including Meridian Works, Blackhorse Lane and Blackhorse Workshop, Barking Arts Live/Work Housing.

Industrial activities are facing increasing housing and land value pressure in "London. Charlton Riverside Employment and Heritage Study," 2017. We Made That for Royal Borough of Greenwich and Greater London Authority. © Photo by Philipp Ebeling.

Logistics and distribution in Charlton, South East London. "Charlton Riverside Employment and Heritage Study," 2017. We Made That for Royal Borough of Greenwich and Greater London Authority. © Photo by Philipp Ebeling.

as a productive city. As the city strives to achieve good growth that benefits its citizens, how can those working in the built environment sustain and support London's strengths as a productive city? London's architects, urban designers, developers, planners, and policy makers are finding new ways of retaining and integrating industry in the city. Through a series of interviews, *London Made* draws on the city's wealth of existing intelligence and expertise to explore what is being done, propositionally and strategically, to support London as a productive city.

London, Annex
Place, Spaces, Work
Publica
The Store Studios

The creative industries are the fastest growing sector of the United Kingdom's economy. This growth is part of an international trend taking place as technology rapidly evolves, and awareness of the economic, social, and civic value of creative work increases.

At the forefront of this evolution is London, one of the world's creative centers. Historically, London has been home to a diverse range of businesses in the creative industries, with leading practitioners in the architecture, design, advertising, film, broadcasting, photography, technology, publishing, cultural, music, and arts and crafts sectors all choosing to make London their home.

From self-employed individual makers, to larger, more established companies, London attracts inventive, talented people whose presence animates streets and neighborhoods and stimulates local economies. The city's mixed stock of buildings has been appropriated and customized again and again to house innovators and allow creative businesses to thrive.

Many of these creative businesses operate in clusters across the inner city. These clusters are integrated into the civic life of London neighborhoods; they are places where creative people meet, build relationships, and share ideas. By clustering together, creative businesses can exchange practical skills and industry knowledge and make connections and deals that allow the creative economy to thrive.

Throughout London's history, elements of the creative industries have tended to be in close proximity to one another, forming cultural quarters through a collective identity and a need for access to shared resources. The character of the buildings and spaces available for creative endeavors has influenced cultural quarters, and in turn, the character of these place continues to be fundamental to the success of the creative industries.

To retain highly skilled talent, London's creative industries require greater recognition from business and political leaders, investment in digital and physical infrastructure, and more spaces for experimentation and growth.

This exhibition reaffirms the value of the creative industries to London and the urgency of maintaining progress by increasing access to networks, spaces, and opportunity.

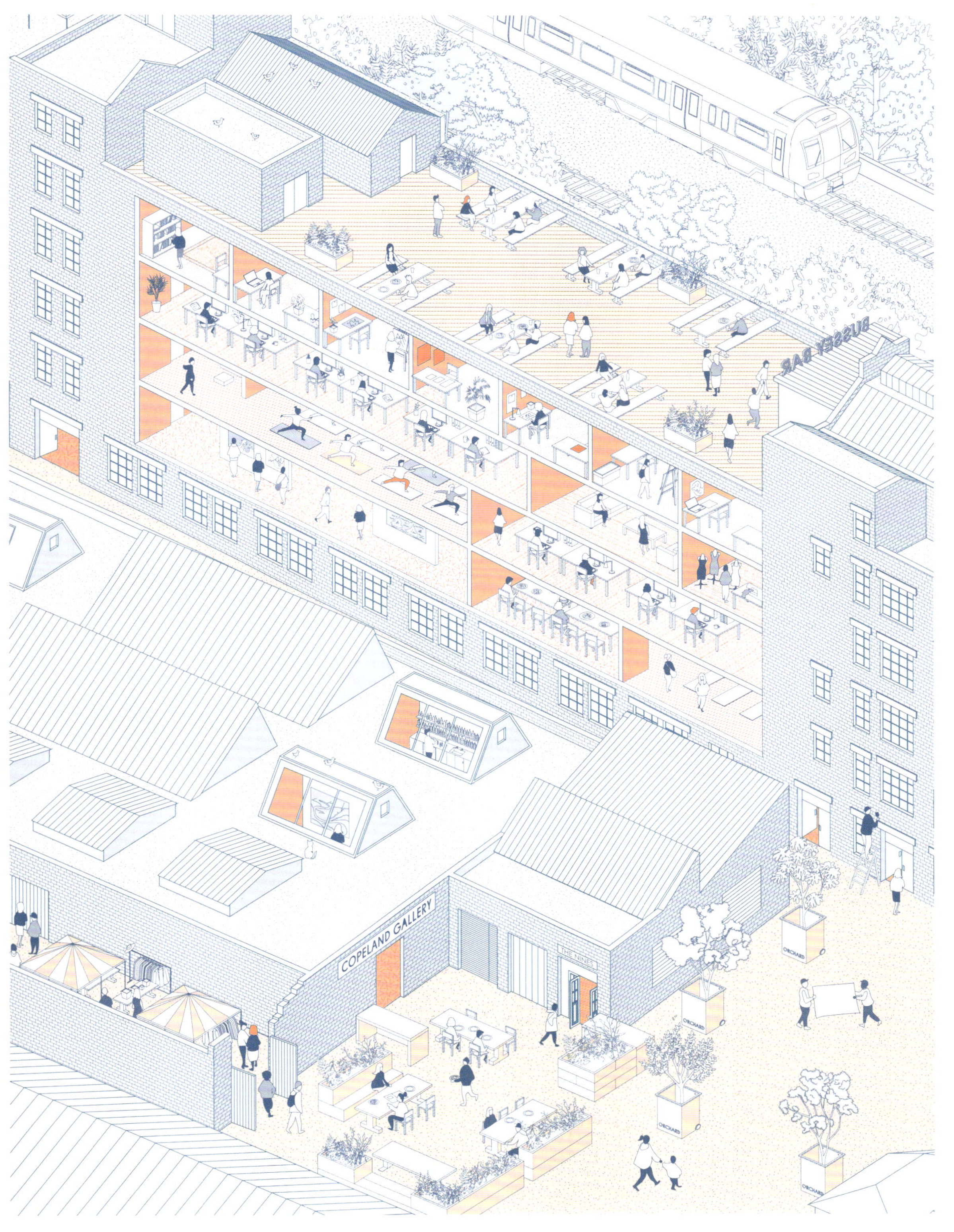

Daytime drawing of activity within the Bussey Building, London. From "Place, Spaces, Work: The Creative Industries" © Publica 2017, all rights reserved.

Macao
Macao Shaped by Use: Formalizing the
Vernacular Customization of the City
Nuno Soares
Filipa Simões

The contemporary city is a complex system where a multitude of factors and dwellers interact, creating a multi-layered spatial structure that supports urban life.

Traditional fields of architectural and urban morphology base their analysis on private and public spaces and on the forms of buildings, blocks, streets, and squares. However, since the city is also a product of its community, it is fundamental to understand how its inhabitants transform and fit it to their individual needs, and how the physical manifestations of these interventions influence urban space.

Macao is a fitting urban reality to study this problematic; it is a densely populated territory where vernacular customization is so intense and widespread that it produces a dramatic impact on the operation and shape of urban space.

Macao Shaped by Use is a spatial installation that displays research on the layer between public and private spaces, more specifically on the shapes that are generated by the customization of public space by its inhabitants. From the urban morphology standpoint, these vernacular customization devices—canopies, annexes, hawker booths, outdoor ads, rooftop houses, and caged windows—are urban elements that, despite their minimal scale, influence the use and shape of the city.

The exhibition is organized in three parts: "Types," "Section," and "Doc." "Types" defines the essential nature, form, and function of each of the six vernacular customization devices studied. "Section" highlights the layer between the public and private domains, displaying the formal variations of the types and their relation within the urban space. "Doc" frames each type of device, documenting their collective impact on Macao's urban landscape.

This installation showcases a typo-morphology essay on these vernacular devices, which will provide a methodological tool for the analysis of such phenomena, both in this and other, similar urban contexts.

First it documents the form of these vernacular devices, highlighting the six types and

Rooftop houses in Macao © Nuno Soares, 2013

categorizing their typological variations. Second it places these vernacular devices within the framework of the architectural discipline, opening new areas for future architectural intervention, formalizing the vernacular customization of the city.

Madrid
DREAMadrid
José Luis Esteban Penelas

"…nothing is more disturbing than the constant movements of what seems motionless."
—Gilles Deleuze

Constructing Dreams of Energy

Welcome to a dream.

Today's metacities are formed by liquid and fluid mechanisms of energy. It is important to understand that the changes that occur due to their collective inhabitants make them capable of mutating at great speed. Cities that appear to be motionless generate a spatial multiplicity; they mirror the paradigm of production (Jean Baudrillard). Today's cities arise as energy cities. They are supercities of today's post-industrial era of supermodernity (Daniel Bell).

Madrid Zero Energy is an example for the twenty-first century. Our proposal is an open dream of the future, developing thoughts and projects, and building up from a human scale to a territorial scale; a zero energy dream where the protagonist is the human being, where the city of Madrid is an example of zero consumption and a healthy citizenry.

Architecture and urbanism are shaped by a complexity of actions, and through these creative actions, subsequent thoughts emerge. They are also poetic. Today's architecture changes at a vertiginous speed, and the way it has been understood for almost the past two thousand years is mutating. The concepts of velocity, spectacle, anonymity, limits, mobility, sustainability, health, and energy define the parameters of today's globalized society.

Madrid: Fresh Air, Zero Consumption, Healthy, *Glo-cal* Madrid

Throughout its history, Madrid has been treasured for its fresh air—a great tradition which is currently being recovered through the actions of zero consumption. This concept is linked to the "commons" of the Seoul Biennale. We are generating a new Madrid Zero Energy. It is understood, in time and space, through communication, through urban and territorial infrastructure (highways, metro, trains, cycling lanes, buses, and green corridors) and through high-speed infrastructure (AVE, the supergeneration of new infrastructures, the real-time transmission of images through mobile phones), all of which are susceptible to being rethought, reanalyzed, and transformed. All of this is aimed toward zero consumption and interactive processes that branch and become interconnected: the city of Madrid.

Madrid is a metacity. Its form is predictable and projectable through new computational energy—systems that make its real-time adaptation possible. The emerging needs of society's communication are met through the strengthening of super-infrastructures.

A rethinking and evolution of the city of Madrid will inevitably keep mutating toward other configurations that express new conditions of this territorial and glo-cal supercity: a city of six million inhabitants, a glo-cal insertion with a common, variable intercultural program that can be altered with the idiosyncrasies of each country, connectable to other cities in the global context.

Computational Zero Energy Systems: Planning Madrid for the Twenty-First Century

Presenting Madrid as a future global city, Madrid Zero Energy is the outcome of continuous research conducted for more than a decade on public urban space and regeneration, and it proposes an "advanced evolution" in urban thinking: "A new profile for twenty-first century cities in an era of super modernity."

The aim of this meta Madrid Zero Energy is to become self-sufficient by 2025, an estimation which, according to research conducted by the municipality, will be possible. The

Energy map in Madrid.

dream is for Madrid to become a city of zero consumption, a new meta energy zero consumption city ("meta" from the Greek meaning "further" and "beyond"). From here we generate a computational intelligent energy system capable of real-life adaptation, based on the development of a fluid network.

Five Energy Concepts
DREAMadrid integrates five strong core concepts into generic public, urban, and metropolitan spaces as part of a global network of similar nodes, where citizens become aware of the environment's performance:
— Future (establishing design as a tool to produce a tangible future)
— Environments and ecology (as constitu-

tive parts of the future)
— Enjoyment (as a productive tool oriented toward sustainability)
— Zero consumption and health (Madrid to become a 100% healthy city)
— Citizens' participation in Madrid will count on citizens' real-time participation

DREAMadrid explores the limits of these mutable scenarios via a shared working methodology based on parallel and co-evolving strategies, and it develops urban strategies based on the growth of Madrid as an almost unique example of the development of a city based on Zero Energy. The vision is propelled by the municipality.

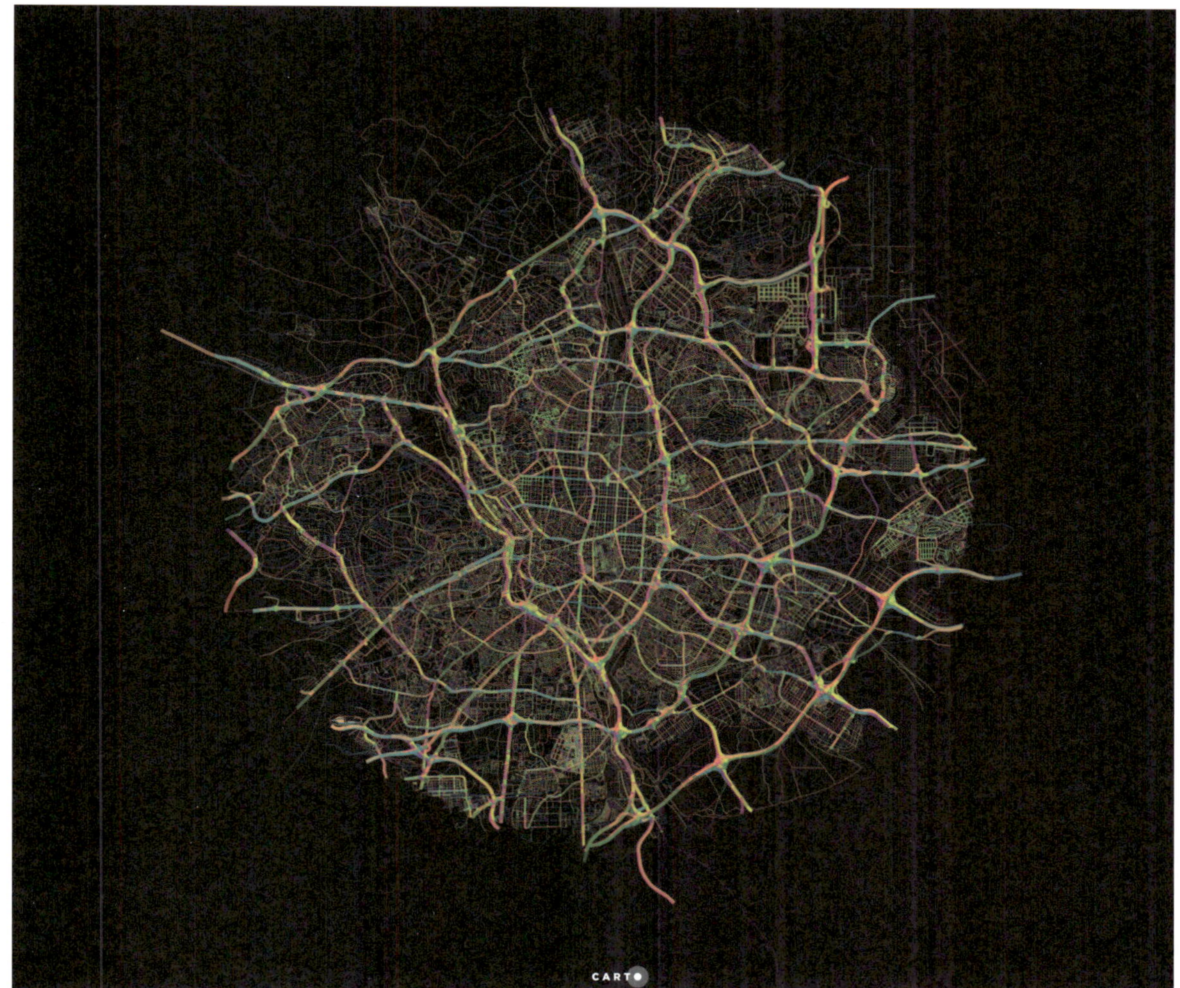

Overlay of energy maps in Madrid.

Future Energy

Our urban areas cannot continue to grow as they have done in the past. In this era of changing demographics and supermodernity (Marc Augé), diminishing resources, and climate change, new models for living are needed. In others words: How can we live in our unstable and fluctuating contemporary cities? *DREAMadrid* explores and presents new models for living in future cities at four scales (human, residential, urban, and territorial) based on health and zero consumption.

DREAMadrid… dreaming the future energy.

Medellín
A City for Life

Jorge Pérez-Jaramillo

Medellín has overcome a deep crisis. Over the past three decades, the city has undergone a remarkable transformation, through collective leadership, and diverse, catalytic urban projects.

Through a broad and complex process of social dialogue, participatory planning, and democratic and institutional evolution, Medellín has overcome extreme rates of inequality, has brought accessibility to the city for all, and has become an urban lab for the construction of public life. The city has accomplished all this with the aim of inclusive and

© Latitud Taller de Arquitectura (Imagen Aerea Medellín), 2017.

sustainable development, using infrastructure, architectural urbanism, and planning as social tools.

The new long-term Land Use Plan for Medellín (POT 2014–2027), proposing a "compact city" model, prioritizes urban development inside the city's urban fabric by identifying thirty-three strategic redevelopment areas. For example, as a botanic park, Medellín River Parks aims to promote green urban development, environmental restoration, social inclusion, and connectivity throughout the city. It also aims to control urban sprawl and promote equitable solutions for the communities located on top of the mountains surrounding the central city, through a Metropolitan Green Belt master plan.

The strategic objective is to develop a sustainable urbanization and to recover the values of our territory and our biodiversity. We aim to bring the river back to the citizens as the main structure of the urban ecosystem by capitalizing on its environmental wealth, and its pollution and smart-water management and control program. Our goal is to optimize its current role as a central corridor for regional and urban multimodal mobility, including non-motorized modes, waterway restoration, and to create quality public spaces and parks for all.

Over the hills, the transformation of water reservoirs from infrastructure into community centers for public life and equality, connecting the people and the cityscape, complements a wide range of public facilities for multimodal transportation, culture, education, and leisure. This transformation inspires hope by restoring public life.

Imminent Commons

The geographical valley is our greatest asset. To reintegrate the city with its natural base is our best option. Medellín faces big challenges and looks forward once more to a new stage of collective work. After an inspiring success story, with strong continuity up to this point, the time has come for its evolution.

Messina
Messina Waterfront Polycenter: A Socio-Economic and Cultural Catalyst
Urban Future Organization

The Messina Waterfront Polycenter was originally envisaged as one of a series of governmental initiatives for urban regeneration interventions associated with the mega-infrastructural development proposal for a new Messina-Reggio Calabria Bridge. The urban plan makes provisions for major upgrades for the national railway network, including relocation of the main railway station for the forthcoming high-speed trains.

The project is conceived as an urban pivot, leading a series of new civic develop-

Messina Waterfront Masterplan. The new urban scheme attempts to address the opportunity to motivate a new urban era for Messina as a series of new reference points in urban landscape and skyline, respecting local density, typography, and environmental factors. The core interest seeks to integrate architectural design with urban ecology, and offer multiple and flexible spatial structure reflecting the much needed flexibility regarding end users, social groups, and operational strategies. © Urban Future Organization

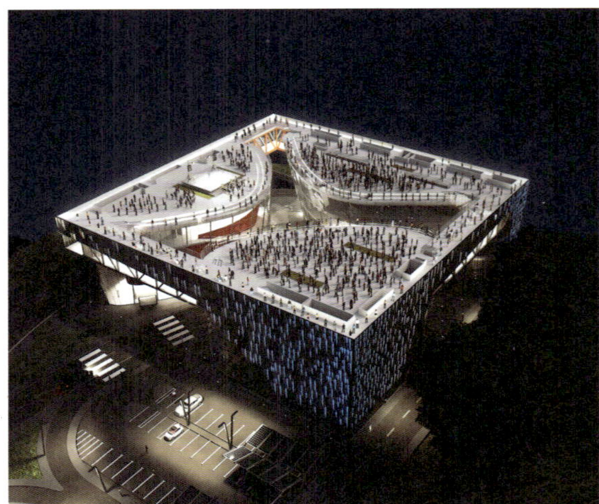

Polycentre. The final version of Polycenter, corresponding to a new development proposal required from Messina Townhall, propose a different typology and strategy. © Urban Future Organization

ments from the historical harbor to the new railway station, including an artificial marina, as part of an ambitious but necessary future plan devised by the municipality. The original winning scheme attempted to motivate a new urban era for Messina as a new reference point in the urban landscape and skyline. The core interest seeks to integrate architectural design with urban ecology and to offer multiple and flexible spatial structures, reflecting a much-needed flexibility regarding end users, social groups, and operational needs.

Following the indefinite suspension of the Messina-Reggio Calabria Bridge project, the Municipality of Messina revisited the original design brief and business plan and subsequently revised the design parameters to reflect a more up-to-date social and economic projection of the city, including a new and more compact volumetric requirement for the project, as well as a new infrastructure and traffic plan. An important road was introduced to cut through the site.

While adhering to the original design principles—to enhance cultural economic prosperity, promote small business entrepreneurship, integrate passive and efficient energy performance, and engage with social enterprises and local stakeholders—the proposal has evolved into a more subtle, condensed, but equally exciting, socio-economic and cultural intervention for the city. It formalizes the tension between spatial fragmentation and experiential coherence through architectural composition, programming, spatial curation, and operational intelligence.

The proposed "tribrid"—facilities management, cultural events, and start-up business training—surrounds a central void, where the spatial tension between the three independent buildings is amplified and celebrated. In order to form new and different relationships between the post-industrial context, rail yards, traffic patterns, and the beautiful but coarse natural cliff side, where conventional street-level engagement is less effective, the design inverts the conventional plinth hierarchy to form a new and elevated public-space level, with minimal street frontage.

From the street, the project shifts the attention to the interior; once visitors are inside, the project shifts the attention back to the exterior, through the central void, to the top floor, and the exciting roof terrace. By the time visitors arrive at the rooftop, the terrace reconnects their architectural experience back to the city of Messina and the sea.

The inverted hierarchy employs the concept of the "deep envelope" to articulate spatial experiences between exteriority and interiority. It unifies all three buildings' services and utilities, as the "central void" leads to the converged top level that promotes productivity and competitiveness. These frame and enhance the introverted spatial relationships with an open public domain, the roof terrace.

In contrast to the convention of street-level public space, the elevated roof terrace celebrates the city. The new interiority and altered ground level shift the attention from street to roof and back to the city with various roof activations at different scales, from observation corners to amphitheatre, from roof gardens to vast open terraces, and more. The project exploits new architectural potentials and urban relationships beyond conventional practice and intelligence, beyond the dialectics of coherence and incongruence. The design cultivates a new autonomy for interiority from exteriority, and a new interdependence between massing objects and void. The tension between section and plan, floor plates and envelope, generates an emerging sense of enclosure.

Mexico City
A Living Laboratory to Prototype: The Future of the Cities We Want
Laboratorio para la Ciudad

A Lab for the Megalopolis

Mexico City is a perfect example of both the promise and the hurdles of the coming urban challenge. It is the largest and oldest urban agglomeration in the Americas, but it has all the problems of an emerging city.

The Lab connects the creative energies of this megalopolis and its twenty-two million inhabitants, in order to inject good ideas back into the city's systems. Places like this give us an opportunity to start exploring and experimenting with solutions for a new urban age, by prototyping in the present what cities of the future will look like.

What Kind of City Do You Want?

Our ethos is to stimulate citizens' imaginations by involving them in larger-scale conversations, which provide us the tools to envision and articulate the city we all want. We imagine a creative, open, playful, and pedestrian-friendly city, where citizens contribute to its creation.

The very first step in our creative process starts with a provocation. More than a simple question, a provocation is a first step toward finding solutions. The aim of this activity is to provoke a new train of thought in which everyone will be able to visualize how people from different countries conceive their ideal cities.

This intervention will allow the attendees of the Seoul Biennale 2017 to experience, through Lab's lenses, the power of collaboration and data visualization. This tangible evidence will enable us to highlight the overlooked connections among different cultures and will show how the differences can contribute to creating what kind of cities we want.

Urban Artifact: A tool with which the LabCDMX intervenes the social fabric in order to attract attention and become a hub — for a specific time window — for discussions, for dialogues, to provoke certain behavior and to do surveys and get to know what people think and see of their City. © 2014, Laboratory for the City, Joel Nuño

Peatoniños Workshop: A series of activities that take place in selected streets in Mexico City in which kids learn and play around the topic of "The Right to the City and Play". These activities are developed based on a Community Centered Design approach. © 2016, Laboratory for the City, Joel Nuño

Mumbai
The Bench-Ladder Conversations: Between Systems and Madness
Rupali Gupte, Prasad Shetty (BARD Studio)

Mumbai's urbanism is shaped through intense negotiations between "systems" that are put in place to regulate the use of urban resources and individual "madness" that pushes itself beyond the boundaries set by these systems. Transactional objects and spaces are born into the context of this intense negotiation, and they significantly shape urban form and life. This work sets up a conversation between systems and madness to put together an understanding of Mumbai's urbanity. *The Bench-Ladder* is one in a series of transactional objects and spaces through which the conversation is made. It is a tool that aids the painter in his work by day, and invites a community to come together and rest by evening.

The mobilization of the idea of "commons" is to discuss any resource calls for its fair use by the people who share it. This "fair use" implies that there is an ordered way of using the resource. For this ordered way to exist, there needs to be a disciplining system. In a city, this system gets worked out as concrete, physical infrastructure like water supply systems or transportation, or as soft, intangible frameworks like laws, customs, or practices. The idea of "commons" invariably requires "systems" in order to manifest itself. The stake raised for the commons appears to be a stake raised for systems. Until now, cities and societies have struggled to set up such systems. The threat to the commons is, then, largely due to the unexpected and deviant behavior of some of the commoners. For example, every country has a particular rule to drive on roads. A driver should keep the car to the left or to the right of the road, depending on which country she is driving in. However, if one wants to explore the possibilities of driving in the opposite direction of this rule, then such a person will be stopped and probably arrested immediately, as such behavior could create tremendous traffic jams, accidents, even a complete breakdown of the transport infrastructure. Here, the "commons" (the road) would be under threat due to the deviant behavior of an individual, as it would limit the access of others to the road.

However, people in the city are full of deviant behavior—their individual "trips." Trying to drive in the opposite direction of the rule, collecting strange objects, behaving like spies, obsessively trying to order things, achieving mundane goals, dismantling equipment, opposing new ideas, and tracking obscure data are practices that go beyond routine. These practices are not useful to produce grand conceptualizations of cities and are often discarded as stray, individual preoccupations. While some of these obsessions are related to earning and occupations, others are simply "useless." But we all seem to have a trip that we live with and for. Trips provide individuals with their energy. Our contention is that such energies cumulatively produce a city. Trips are absurd quests, unusual obsessions. and bizarre interests that seem to be making the city. The city seems to be acquiring its generative energy from such trips. In many ways the city seems to be a madhouse, and

the inmates seems to be running it. As trips produce "deviant behavior" in individuals, they are usually in contradiction to the world of systems. While systems demand sanity and uniformity, trips push for madness and personality. However, systems and madness should not be considered as opposed to each other; it was probably some trip that created the first system. Nevertheless, the stakes raised for commons then appear to be pushing out the stakes for madness.

Our studies from Mumbai show that it is in this context that transactional objects and spaces are born. They negotiate the tensions between "commons" and "trips"— or "systems" and "madness"—by increasing the transactibility of urban form (here, the distinct physicality of urban space). These transactional objects and spaces appropriate systems, orders, and infrastructure to allow for trips and madness to flourish. In the physical world of urban form, they manifest themselves in many ways, including extension to shops, folding shops of street vendors, porting devices, resting apparatus, fixtures fixed on boundary walls that help occupy them, things used to claim space, or orphaned furniture left for wanderers. However, these are not just utilized to facilitate transactions; they are quirky, erotic, sedimented, and absurd. In their absurdity these are instances of dreams trying to take shape and aspira-

Poky sphere, 2015. © BARD Studio

The Bench-Ladder Conversations, 2015. © BARD Studio

tions trying to get worked out. Conventional design practices require a certain fixity and a clear set of measurable parameters, and their anticipatory capacity usually only exists to the extent of the parameters that are taken into consideration while designing. Therefore, design practices often find themselves in an awkward position with respect to the logic of the city that throw up newer challenges. As manifestations of intense negotiations, the transactional objects and spaces are often able to quickly respond to complicated, newer challenges thrown up by cities. They are agile and are under constant transformation, which is often incremental, sporadic, and based on parameters that are beyond the detection of empirical methods.

Oslo
Edible Oslo
Transborder Studio

Norway's capital city, Oslo, is placed between two large and diverse organic landscapes—the fjord and the forest. These biotopes represent an important and underused resource for the city. Oslo, like many other cities, is full of edible plants and species that for different reasons we do not harvest, eat, or take in use; instead, we let them go unexploited. The reason for this could be a lack of information or tradition for our local edible inventory, combined with a strong economy. The choices we make today about which organisms to eat are derived from the biological knowledge of long ago. In the past, natural scientific illustrations were a record of the identities of living things and were the medium to inform people of the existence of species. The agenda for our project is to unveil the hidden potentials found in the fauna and flora of Oslo and to connect them to a growing network of urban food producers. Combining botanical art and mapping, the installation records the edible creatures and plants of Oslo as well as local producers, showing a never-before presented portrait of the city.

We live in a time when agriculture has a new relevance related to urban food culture,

bio products, and the agricultural sector's role in a sustainable future. Our goal is to highlight this new interest and show that its development can become a reinterpretation of the historic relationship between the city and its productive surroundings.

Paris
Réinventer Paris
Pavillon de l'Arsenal

As an unprecedented challenge launched by the City of Paris for designers, urban operators, and investors from all walks of life, the Call for Innovative Urban Projects *Réinventer Paris* is a world first in aiming to imagine and build the city of tomorrow differently. For a year, twenty-three sites[5] and properties be-

5. Hôtel particulier Bûcherie (Bûcherie Townhouse), Hôtel particulier Villiers (Villiers Townhouse), Piat, Buzenval, Gare Masséna (Masséna Station), Sous-station Voltaire (Voltaire Substation), Ordener, Bains-Douches Castagnary (Castagnary Bath-Shower), Bessières, Gambetta, Hôtel de Coulanges, Morland, Edison, Italie, Ancien Conservatoire (Former Conservatory), Pitet Curnonsky, Pershing, Ternes-Villiers, Poterne des Peupliers, Ourcq-Jaurès, Paris Rive Gauche (The Left Bank), Triangle Évangile, Clichy-Batignolles.

longing to the city government were offered to these professionals so that they could express their talent and develop exceptional projects.

More than 800 teams from fifteen different nationalities consisting of architects, landscape designers, urban planners, real estate stakeholders, and engineers, as well as farmers, chefs, anthropologists, artists, philosophers, fashion designers, entrepreneurs, energy companies, associations, residents, and so on rethought ways to create projects and to seek the keys to a new language of urban and architectural design.

Innovations, whether social, architectural, environmental, technological, legal, financial, or in construction or customary, emerged in all kinds of forms and at all stages of construction and use. Aquaponics, participatory housing, co-construction, nudge, reuse of materials, decontamination, new materials (vegetal or photovoltaic concrete, bio-facades, paper bricks, active slabs), urban farms, co-fooding, co-working, or co-living spaces, third-places, urban campsites, are some of

Edible Oslo, 2017. © Soyoung Lee

the many proposals submitted, at times combining together multiple innovations.

The winners presented in this exhibition showcase this extraordinary abundance of ideas, as well as the enthusiasm aroused among both private developers who had acquired land within Paris and the city's various *arrondissements* (municipal subdivisions) in order to rethink the traditional modes of action, to invent completely new processes, and to introduce new methods to imagining the Paris of tomorrow.

Réinventer Paris is committed to the development of 150,000 square meters, including more than 1,300 homes, 60,000 square meters of co-working spaces and offices, four hotels and three youth hostels, a swimming pool, and more 26,000 square meters of planted areas.

Morland, mixité capitale (Morland, a Capital Mix): Building a Mixed and Shared City

The transformation of the old administrative center in the heart of Paris makes it possible to invent a new type of mixed building on a very large scale. The program covers over 40,000 square meters, combining social and private-market housing units, offices, co-working spaces, a hotel, a youth hostel, a swimming pool, an art center, a food market, and a public belvedere with a panoramic view designed by the artist Olafur Eliasson.

La ville multi-strates (Multilevel City): Transforming Infrastructure

Paris innovates by developing new modes of transport such as Vélib' (bike sharing program), Autolib' (electric car sharing), Cityscoot (electric scooter rental), driverless cars, and more. This mutation is accompanied by a transformation of road infrastructure, including bicycle paths, bus lanes, and embankment roads. As both a work of an art and a public park, "La ville multi-strates" is a bridge set above the city's main ring road, developing a new centrality and creating, alongside the "Mille arbres" (A Thousand Trees) project, a new landscape with rooftop tree planting.

L'îlot fertile (The Fertile Island): Making a Zero-Carbon Neighborhood

The Paris Climate and Energy Action Plan will reduce greenhouse gas emissions in the Paris region by 75% in 2050 compared to 2004. As a major consumer of energy, the building sector is contributing to this ambition. "L'îlot fertile" aims to build an environmentally "virtuous" mixed neighborhood (more than 400 homes and 9,000 square meters of green space), setting the standard for urban ecology and energy transition, with the goal of achieving zero carbon status throughout the life of the neighborhood and significant reduction in greenhouse gases.

Tranches de vie (Slices of Life): Foster Inclusive Development

Fostering participatory design, Paris affirms its desire to seek a profound change in the art of designing the city. Driven by its future inhabitants and designers, this project combines private and social housing units, a nursery and urban agriculture. Put together, they create the conditions for a sharing economy that aims to pool resources in order to fully integrate the building into its urban and social environment.

In Vivo: Integrate Architecture with Biotechnology

"In Vivo" creates an active bio-facade for the first time in Paris. This protective building shell allows the production of microalgae for the healthcare and research markets. This experimental project includes classical and other housing units for researchers, as well as an open access laboratory for citizen-driven biotechnology on the ground floor.

Stream Building: Inventing Tomorrow's Office

The "Stream Building" aims to prefigure the hybrid building of tomorrow by layering restaurants, services, co-working spaces, and an innovative hotel on the upper floors. The project is based on an evolutionary wooden structure that houses various programs divided into four major areas responding to different times of the day in order to ensure the building's occupancy 24/7: Stream Work/Stream Stay/ Stream Eat/Stream Play.

Réalimenter Masséna (Re-feed Masséna): Promoting the Circular Economy

Driven by the principles of the circular economy and micro-economy, "Ré-alimenter Masséna" proposes an innovative program housed in a wooden construction that combines housing units, cultural spaces, as well as spaces dedicated to issues concerning food: its production, mediation, and sales. This inclusive place, where one can live and cultivate as well as be cultivated, aims to contribute to inventing the tools necessary for elaborating a new relationship with a sustainable and resilient countryside.

Le Philanthro-Lab (The Philanthro-Lab): Activate New Uses

Innovative for both its program and design, "Le Philanthro-Lab" is a unique place of encounter and sharing. As the first incubator dedicated to philanthropy, this information and training space is committed to welcoming sponsors or volunteers who wish to engage with individual organizations, as well as project developers who want to enrich their knowledge, improve their projects, and make their work known. Its new architecture is emblematic of the transformative potential of this historic monument, which was established as a medical school in the fifteenth century.

Bains douches & Co (Bath-Shower & Co): Stimulating the Existing

The existing bath-shower site on rue Castagnary illustrates the city's ability to rebuild itself while respecting its historical landscape. Operating as a casino in 1890, a cinema in 1908, and then a bath-shower site in the early 1930s, the building is preparing for redevelopment today. The project combines a co-working space in the rehabilitated section, and a colocation space in the newly constructed section, a structure that is innovative in its wooden construction as well as its use.

Le jardin habité (The Inhabited Garden): Repair Large Housing Complexes

"Le jardin habité" invests in the new right-of-ways created by reorganizing access to the housing units and open spaces of a large housing complex from the 1970s. The three buildings, with clear sculpted silhouettes, align with the streets to articulate these new public spaces and those of the existing property complexes. Through these largely vegetative facades, thanks to the installation of a light mesh as a means for climbing plants, the inhabited garden project also aims to recreate continuity with the surrounding neighborhood.

Le relais Italie (Relay Italy): Adapt rather than Demolish

The carbon footprint of rehabilitation projects is fifteen times less than that of demolition-reconstruction. Accordingly, the team behind "Le relais Italie" proposes to keep the structure of the old conservatory that is on the site and to extend it. "Le relais Italie" combines co-working spaces, a café-restaurant, and cultural spaces in the existing building, and houses a student residence over three floors in the wooden section. The result is a project that synergistically layers different functions with one another: habitat, leisure, work, culture, and social activities.

Node: Valuing the Neglected

"Node" brings together two programs in a signal building at the entrance to the city: an urban delivery logistics space and a funeral space. The first program, dedicated to responding to the "last kilometer" problem of supply-chain management, proposes a metropolitan-scale logistics space that aims to transport goods that enter and circulate in Paris in optimum conditions via clean vehicles. The second program, designed to accommodate grieving families with attention and dignity, provides a funeral space that includes ceremonial and citizen-friendly rooms, as well as all the necessary technical equipment. A central, shared garden, favoring remembrance, ensures the peaceful coexistence of the two programs.

Étoile Voltaire: Revealing Industrial Heritage

Employing reversible interventions and built on the foundations of the circular economy, "Étoile Voltaire" fits into the existing framework of the electrical substation at Parmentier, to offer this dynamic district the cinema

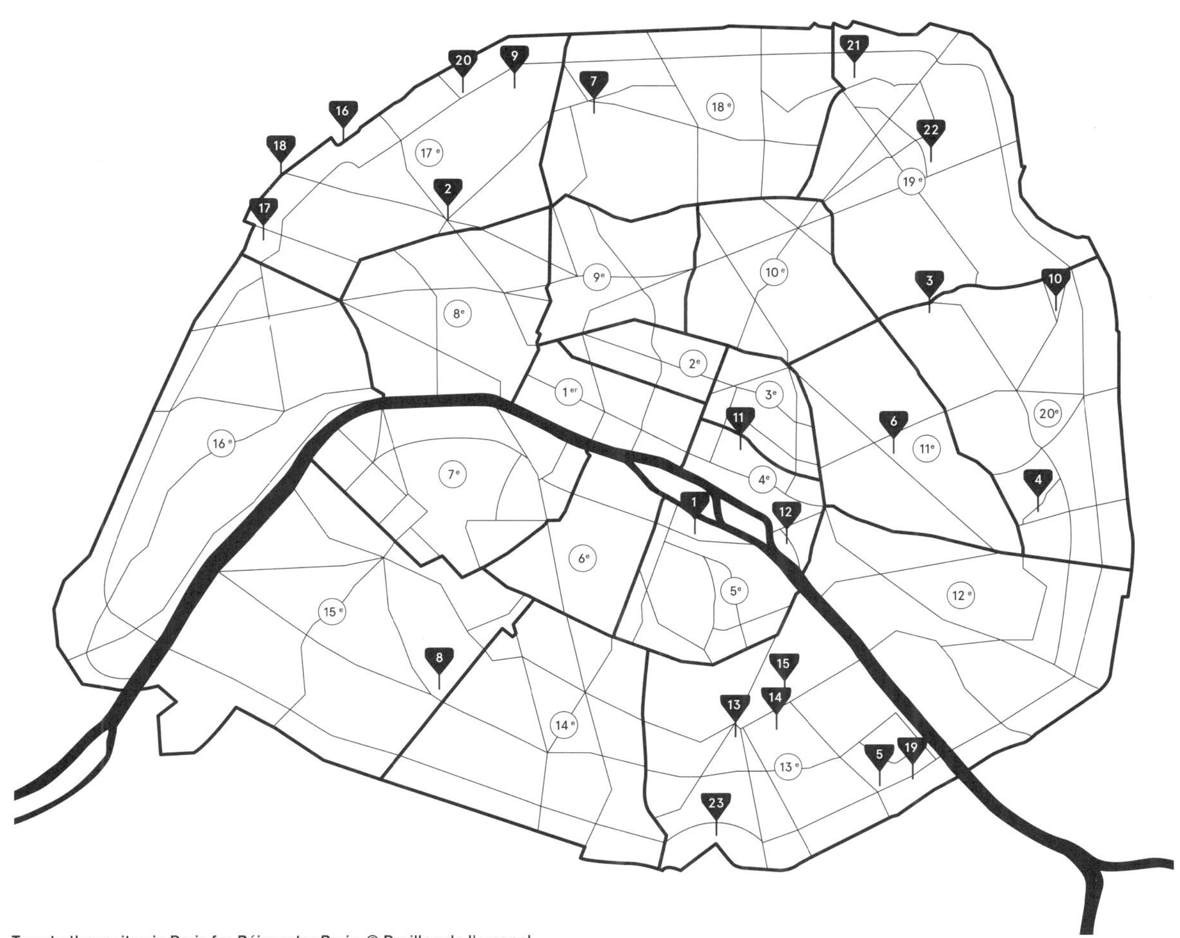

Twenty-three sites in Paris for *Réinventer Paris*. © Pavillon de l'arsenal

that it lacks. Responding to the challenge of redeveloping the industrial heritage of Paris, its architecture, and its volumes, the project proposes to extend the existing building with a cinema space overlooking the roofs of Paris, to annouce the new identity of this exceptional building.

NOC (Not Only a Campus) 42: Developing Student Housing 2.0

The Parisian school known simply as "42" offers an alternative education in the field of computer programming that is freely accessible to students, with no diploma required. Despite its educational success and the international recognition it has garned, many of 42's enrolled students have given up their places since they lack the means to live in Paris. This project offers these students a low-cost accommodation solution that reinvents the traditional dormitory to provide sleeping spaces that are adapted to the lifestyles of contemporary students, while offering a high degree of comfort despite the crowded accommodations.

Collectif Coulanges—Mode création et design (Collectif Coulanges—Fashion, Creation, and Design): Collecting Creative Energies

In the heart of the historic district of the Marais, in an *hôtel particulier* (grand townhouse) where the Marquise de Sévigné, a famous seventeenth-century writer, spent her youth, the "Collectif Coulanges" project, driven by players in the fashion industry, finds its dynamism by combining three typological models: activity hub, collaborative/entrepreneurial

The Rail Farm. © Corentin Perrichot

space, and the concept or pop-up store. Integration of the program's cultural character with the history and patrimony of the building—as well as the project's economic ambitions—invents a unique place for creation that surely contributes to the attractiveness of the neighborhood and to Paris as a whole.

Edison Lite: Re-examine Co-ownership
The "Edison Lite" housing scheme offers several major innovations, from its construction (featuring a three-sided concrete-wood-metal structure), to its high percentage of shared spaces, representing more than 30% of the total living area (including a cellar-workshop and a rooftop vegetable garden), to its pro-

posal to involve the future residents in the design, production, and management of its "tailor-made housing." Moreover, the building is meant to achieve "zero fees" in co-ownership expenses thanks to the income generated from its rental spaces.

Italik: Investing New Right-of-ways
Designed collaboratively in consultation with local residents, "Italik" is established on an almost non-existent plot, which is the residue of a project to widen Avenue d'Italie that was planned as part of the urban transformation of the sector Italie XIII, but not realized. Adjacent to one of the biggest shopping centers in Paris, the project develops alternative commer-

cial facilities for the neighborhood residents, offering them local stores and innovative services.

Mille Arbres (A Thousand Trees): Living on the Ring Road

"Mille Arbres" aims to offer a new skyline for Paris. At a time when some want to build 1,000-meter towers, the team of Japanese architect Sou Fujimoto proposes to plant 1,000 trees over a main Parisian motorway. The project aims to offer a new ecosystem for this automotive urban environment. The entire package includes several programs: a bus station, food court, and children's play space on the ground floor; a public park; offices and hotels on the upper floors; social housing units; and then on the roof, a private domain among the trees.

La ferme du rail (The Rail Farm): Encouraging Urban Agriculture

"La ferme du rail" is a meeting space for urban agriculture, a place for training, accommodation, and food production. It is built around a community of people committed to social integration and horticulture students; developing its gardening activities with direct distribution to consumers, along with utilizing the organic wastes of the city. Its objective is to minimize the usage of energy, food, and financial resources, by implementing a circular economy. "La ferme du rail" also aims to integrate vulnerable people by generating service and agricultural-production jobs.

La fabrique de la danse (Dance Factory): Reinvest in Car Parks

"Dance Factory" proposes to convert a neglected parking facility into an exemplary building of 2,500 square meters. The program supports artistic creation both within the neighborhood and the city at large. The project hopes to encourage innovation in dance and to democratize choreography. The atypical spaces of the old parking facility are thus enhanced: the basement hosts a connected scene and a home for artists. The green roof offers an experimental laboratory for urban ecosystems.

Auberge Buzenval (Buzenval Hostel): Offer a New Type of Hotel

"Auberge Buzenval" has developed a new type of hotel capable of accommodating a broad public and thus allowing mixed occupancy. Thirty-two rooms and seven apartments offer travelers, as well as young people, families, and Parisians at large, a new place dedicated to hospitality and meeting spaces. This new multi-room hotel—offering accommodations ranging from private bedrooms to dormitories—also establishes a strong connection with the immediate neighborhood by making the roof terrace accessible to all, and by promoting the permeability of the ground floor, which is open to the street.

La serre habitée—Archiculture urbaine (The Inhabited Greenhouse—Urban Archiculture): Co-design and Co-build

"La serre habitée" symbolizes the city's commitment to local-level social solidarity and its support for participatory, community-based self-managed projects. Having signed the responsible charter, twenty-four architecture students collectively undertake to co-conceive and then to live and invest in this new social housing residence, located not far from their school, and whose collaborative projects will be open to the surrounding neighborhood. "La serre habitée" thus proposes to develop an alternative model of social housing that is both a means toward—and an outcome of—a collective and sustainable undertaking.

Pyongyang
Pyongyang Sallim

Dongwoo Yim
Calvin Chua

Pyongyang Sallim is a multi-angled exhibition that illuminates the everyday life of Pyongyang residents. Recently, Pyongyang has gradually been introduced to a market economy. The result has been a steady growth of the *donju* (new middle class) population, and a demand for new housing. To meet the demand of the emerging middle class, new apartment complexes are steadily being constructed. One of the core socialist concepts from the past for

© Dongwoo Yim

urban housing development was the "micro district" based on small-scale neighborhood planning, the basis on which housing complexes were built. Today, this ideologically sanctioned framework is being abandoned in order to fulfill a new, more urgent housing demand—that of the emerging middle class. *Pyongyang Sallim* introduces a model home based on an actual apartment complex in Pyongyang, allowing viewers a holistic experience of the lives of Pyongyang residents.

The goal of urban planning in post-war Pyongyang, which was all but burned to the ground during the Korean War, was to build an ideal socialist city. Under this plan, a residential complex would be basically a self-sufficient unit, a self-contained building block from the perspective of the whole city. By building manufacturing facilities and securing green zones within the city, urban planners in Pyongyang tried to realize socialist values in the organization of its urban spaces. Thanks to these efforts, Pyongyang prevented indiscriminate urban sprawl, pursued equality of spaces in the city, allowed for communities to be formed, and enabled production and consumption to take place at the level of the small districts. This was the overall framework of urban planning in Pyongyang from the 1950s to the 1970s, the post-Korean War reconstruction period.

However, beginning in the 1980s and continuing through the 1990s, the North Korean regime began using architecture as propaganda; this is reflected in how apartment buildings were constructed during this period. Representative of residential construction from this period are the Gwangbok (Independence) Street and Tongil (Unification) Street high-rise apartments, well known even to foreigners. The high-rise buildings on these streets not only fulfilled the demand for extra-large apartment units in Pyongyang, but they were also fully utilized as regime propaganda. What is worth paying attention to is that even in these large apartment complexes, the small-district residential framework was, at least formally, maintained. They have within them, for example, child-care facilities, schools, service facilities, and domestic production facilities. Thus, the overall framework for micro-district

residential planning was maintained for over fifty years in Pyongyang.

In more recent years, this overall framework has been seriously undermined. Since the leadership change in 2011, a market economy has been partially but steadily introduced into North Korea. As a result, North Korean people's lives—and in particular the lives of Pyongyang residents, who comprise a special class—clearly began to change. People now use personal smart phones and more automobiles are visible on the streets. Along with the development of markets, where freedom of transactions is guaranteed, the use of credit cards is allowed. North Korean society is changing in these and many other respects, all of which are evidence that a new class of people—that is, a middle class with cash power—is emerging in Pyongyang.

Construction of new apartment buildings in Pyongyang over the past five years was a means of fulfilling the desires of this new economic class. Building an ideal socialist society with micro-district urban planning is no longer a priority; what is now important is the fulfillment of the desires and demands of the new economic class. What they want are better locations, better views, more floor space, and fancier interiors. Accordingly, the recently completed apartment complexes at Ryeomyeong Street and Mirae Scientist Street show the stark contrast between the values Pyongyang is currently pursuing and the values it is abandoning.

It is precisely these apartments where *Pyongyang Sallim* focuses its attention, for these apartments represent an inflection point in Pyongyang's urban planning paradigm. Surely, the new apartments are not representative of the average residential environment in Pyongyang; however, as mentioned, the significance of the new apartment construction in Pyongyang is that it represents a shift in the residential planning framework from that of the past fifty years to a new paradigm. Again, *Pyongyang Sallim* focuses its attention not on the average home, either past or present, but on the direction of a changing Pyongyang and its future. Furthermore, a home shows more than a space where a person lives; it reflects a complex combination of the larger culture, customs, and preferences. With this in mind, *Pyongyang Sallim* has installed a model house so that exhibition visitors may gain a multivalent understanding of the life of Pyongyang residents.

Overall, there are four rooms in *Pyongyang Sallim*: the entrance and living room, a dining room, the kitchen, and finally the bedroom. The size of each room has been adjusted to fit the exhibition module. While the various household items are sourced directly from North Korea, the various articles of furniture have been custom-made for the exhibition. More specifically, furniture, wallpaper, flooring, and lighting have been custom-made to reproduce a sample apartment in Pyongyang. Shoes, clothes, snack foods, and other items were bought locally in North Korea then brought to Seoul. It is expected that viewers in Seoul will be able to experience what is different and what is similar about residential spaces in Seoul and Pyongyang.

Each room contains relevant material on the themes of history, culture, housing, and change. Thus, viewers will not only *experience* a North Korean home, but will also find various informational materials on North Korea and Pyongyang. Historically themed materials focus not only on Pyongyang in the context of the Korean Peninsula's history, but also on the history of Pyongyang's development as a socialist city in the post-Korean War era. Materials on the cultural theme focus on the lives of Pyongyang residents; they also deal with culture in Pyongyang as seen through the eyes of foreign visitors. Materials on housing show various styles of residential architecture, including low-rise, mid-rise, and high-rise apartment buildings. Lastly, materials on the theme of change focus on showing the new development projects that are altering the face of Pyongyang. Photographs, maps, and diagrams as well as architectural models are used to communicate the information effectively. This visual exhibition material is positioned in a manner that fits seamlessly into the composition of the model house so as to not disturb the experience of visiting an apartment.

The apartment unit featured in *Pyongyang Sallim* is modeled after a unit in one of the most recently completed luxury apartment complexes in Pyongyang. These apartments are usually reserved exclusively for Party officers or university faculty members, with amenities not available in most homes in Pyongyang. *Pyongyang Sallim* shows where residential development in Pyongyang is headed with further liberalization of its currently limited market system. What viewers experience at *Pyongyang Sallim* is what would be the most intimate space in a nation that is the most veiled on earth. What they will experience is less representative of Pyongyang as a whole rather than a certain slice of it.

Reykjavík
The Hot Pot as Political Arena

Arna Mathiesen
April Arkitekter

Throughout Iceland, and especially in the capital of Reykjavík, one is never far from a "heitur pottur" or hot pot—a public vessel, scaled to accommodate only a few people at a time, that is filled with hot water fed from easily accessible geothermal reserves. Usually situated within swimming and recreational complexes, hot pots are special moments of physical and social intensity within cities, towns, and landscapes. No matter their context, they stand apart as focal points with a unique cultural significance. They provide literal points of heat and texture in the environment, and they catalyze moments of reflection and communication, relieving dark winter days with intimate moments of warmth. Like a neighborhood pub in other cultures, hot pots draw people from all walks of life, friends and strangers alike, all stripped of their uniforms, together in a beautiful environment of sounds and senses, where eye contact is almost unavoidable. The hot pot is a site of exchange. Interactions that arise include everything from personal rendezvous to political debates.

The size and shape of the first public hot pot in Reykjavík was inspired by the hot spring on Reykholt farm, where Snorri Sturluson (1179–1241), a prominent lawmaker and scholar, lived. Snorri's assassination marked the end of the Icelandic commonwealth and its unique decentralized rule, which arose after the settlement of Iceland in the ninth century. We imagine that Snorri soaked in his proto-hot pot for long hours, reflecting and debating with anyone who joined him in the extraordinary and intimate space—perfectly scaled by nature for one conversation to unfold between people in a vulnerable state—naked and open to nature, but protected by enclosure and warmth.

The "reyk" of Reykholt and Reykjavík refers to the steam emitted from hot springs. Reykjavík has the largest geothermal heating system in the world, heating buildings as well as hot pots. After the 2008 crash, the city of Reykjavík didn't close down a single hot pot, but fortunately built even more of them. The natural heating system, however, is under threat, as the public utility that administers the geothermal reservoirs of the capital region is now also invested in the production of electricity, an industry that has doubled in Iceland since the turn of the century.

Amid rapid urban development and foreign investment/exploitation, the production of electricity from geothermal resources is causing both environmental harm and social detriment. Poorly designed and managed sites compromise drinking water reserves and air quality, and Reykjavíkians are subsidizing private energy and engineering companies that strive to greenwash the global aluminum industry. Citizens confront rising prices for heating and electricity, not to mention entrance fees to hot pots. As the veins in the rocks empty, they take hundreds of years to refill with hot water. New and deeper boreholes need to be drilled to fulfill contracts with international corporations who operate coastal smelters that consume over 80% of the total electricity supply. If the massive drilling continues, it is doubtful that the geothermal reserves of the capital area will last more than fifty years. Reykjavík will lose its natural wonder and, with it, the vibrant culture of the geothermal hot pot. It is a myth that geothermal is renewable—it is not! Yet Reykjavík applied for and won the Nordic Council Nature and Environment Prize in 2014 for "its conscious work on the environmentally friendly use of water and production of district heating and electricity from geothermal energy."

A pipeline channeling geothermal water from the vicinity of Reykjavík to the Hellisheiði power plant.

A public hot pot in Reykjavík, the capital city of Iceland. © April Arkitekter

Our installation invites a reflection on the (im)balance between, on the one hand, the harvesting and use of local natural resources and, on the other hand, the practice of trading resources between geopolitical entities in the age of globalization. The recent history of economic meltdown in Iceland and the ongoing global environmental crisis frame our thinking, and our Hot Pot embraces apparently conflicting trajectories: the human scale of togetherness and interconnectedness confronts the almost absurd scale of the stars. As we soak together, lean back, and look up to the stars, we contemplate harvesting the far reaches of the universe for resources to save us from our self-destructive waste and irresponsibility, as if another chance will make a difference.

Rome
The Theaters of Culture: Ephemeral Projects for the Eternal City
Pippo Ciorra
MAXXI

This exhibit, coordinated by Rome's National Museum of the Twenty-First Century Arts (MAXXI) for the Cities Exhibition in the Seoul Biennale, is a speculation about three major topics. The first topic—undoubtedly the least faithful to the curatorial program of the Seoul exhibition—is an investigation into the possible existence of something we may call European architecture. To investigate the potential of architecture in relation to the cultural industry of the city of Rome today, we chose to involve not only the "Roman" or Italian archi-

tects, but also a selection of five young teams selected through a European Union-funded program for the promotion of young talent in architecture. The program is carried out by a network of eighteen European architectural institutions and is called the Future Architecture Platform. It aims to fuel new voices and to produce radical research on the future of architecture, cities, and landscapes. The five teams involved in the project for the Seoul Biennale, with roots in five different European countries, share both a strong interest in investigating how innovative architectural strategies can have an impact on the future of our cities as well as a deep knowledge of the problems affecting Western urban culture. Here we are probably looking for some kind of generative bottom-up effect, from small to extra-large: we opened up the Rome context of relations between culture, economy, and architecture to the European scene of ideas about architecture and then brought this approach to the attention of the kind of global audience that will be visiting the Seoul Biennale. This is, in our view, a potentially fruitful process, exactly because we consider Seoul a perfect context. This city is where Eastern (sometimes uncontrolled) energy and speed meet a new consciousness—somehow arrived at earlier in Europe—with a need to rethink the concepts of growth, urbanization, and the social role of architecture. The link we generated between young European talent and the Biennale scene looks like a beautiful device to produce a productive clash between the megacity of Seoul and small Euro-practices with a strong view to the future. Rome stands in the middle of this process, aiming to make the best of both points of view: the apparent Eastern easiness in building multiple relations between architecture and socio-economic growth and the oblique, neo-avant-garde, conflictive approach of small-scale teams, intellectually engaged in the building of a new, open, eco-friendly, socio-conscious, techno-mature Europe.

The second topic has mostly to do with how the history of cities is in itself a catalog of surprising suggestions and solutions for today's problems, and with how an original way of looking back to the past can be an extremely productive method of designing the new and the sustainable. In the late 1970s, Rome was a tough city. Criminal and political violence dominated the scene; political terrorism and poorly thought out responses from the state were leaving casualties on the ground every other day. As a result of these conditions, public life—when it was not motivated by the masses or driven by strong political matters—was at its lowest point, with "normal" people scared of walking around in the streets. In 1975, a center-left coalition won local elections for the first time. It chose the most important Italian art historian, Giulio Carlo Argan, to be mayor. Argan, typically a non-registered supporter of the Communist party (an "indipendente di sinistra" or leftist independent), appointed a young and "rebel" architect, Renato Nicolini, born in 1942, as chancellor for culture. Nicolini's solution to bring culture back to life in the city was extremely innovative and still stands as a turning point in many "histories" of architecture, urban life, politics, art, culture, and more. His proposal, developed with a group of extremely creative intellectuals, was quite bold: for the whole summer, nearly all cultural activities should leave their official venues and invade urban space. The starting event was shocking: a gigantic piece of white fabric was suspended between the arches of the Basilica of Maxentius, within the precinct of the formerly "untouchable" Foro Romano (Roman Forum), and 10,000 seats were placed in front of it for a cinema festival. Attendance was way beyond expectations (and also beyond the number of seats); this marked the beginning of a new era, when culture in the city started to take the form of "events" (like the Biennale), when urban architecture took the form of temporary ("ephemeral") constructions, when the power of the masses was diverted from the politics of violence to the politics of culture. "Estate Romana" (Roman Summer) was the beginning of a story that is still going on, consisting of a million summer festivals and events around the world, of new professionals (event planners, "eventologists"), of architectural installations around cities and museums, of never-ending discussions pro or against "ephemeral" projects. But the strongest legacy for us—and for the process

that led to this curatorial project—lies in the eight years when it was managed directly by Nicolini, and in how it invaded the city, bringing cultural life outside the walls of traditional venues within the "centro storico" (historic center). Estate Romana included for the first time the "periferia" (urban periphery—formerly the space of Pier Paolo Pasolini's love and complaint for its subculture) in the cultural life of Rome. The five projects displayed in the installation make a direct reference to a specific episode of Estate Romana. In 1979, Nicolini asked Franco Purini, a prominent architect on the Italian scene, to give a clear urban form to his ambition to "include" the periphery in the cultural arena. Purini chose four strategic sites around the center and made each of them the selected space for music, dance, theater, and media through "ephemeral" architectural projects, still keeping the space for cinema as a focal point in the archeological zone. These four points marked the new "Parco Centrale" (Central Park), and architecture was given a clear and "monumental" role in this process. This is a role we have been trying to revive,

Partial reconstruction of the "Teatrino Scientifico," Franco Purini and Laura Thermes, 2017. © Courtesy of Fondazione MAXXI

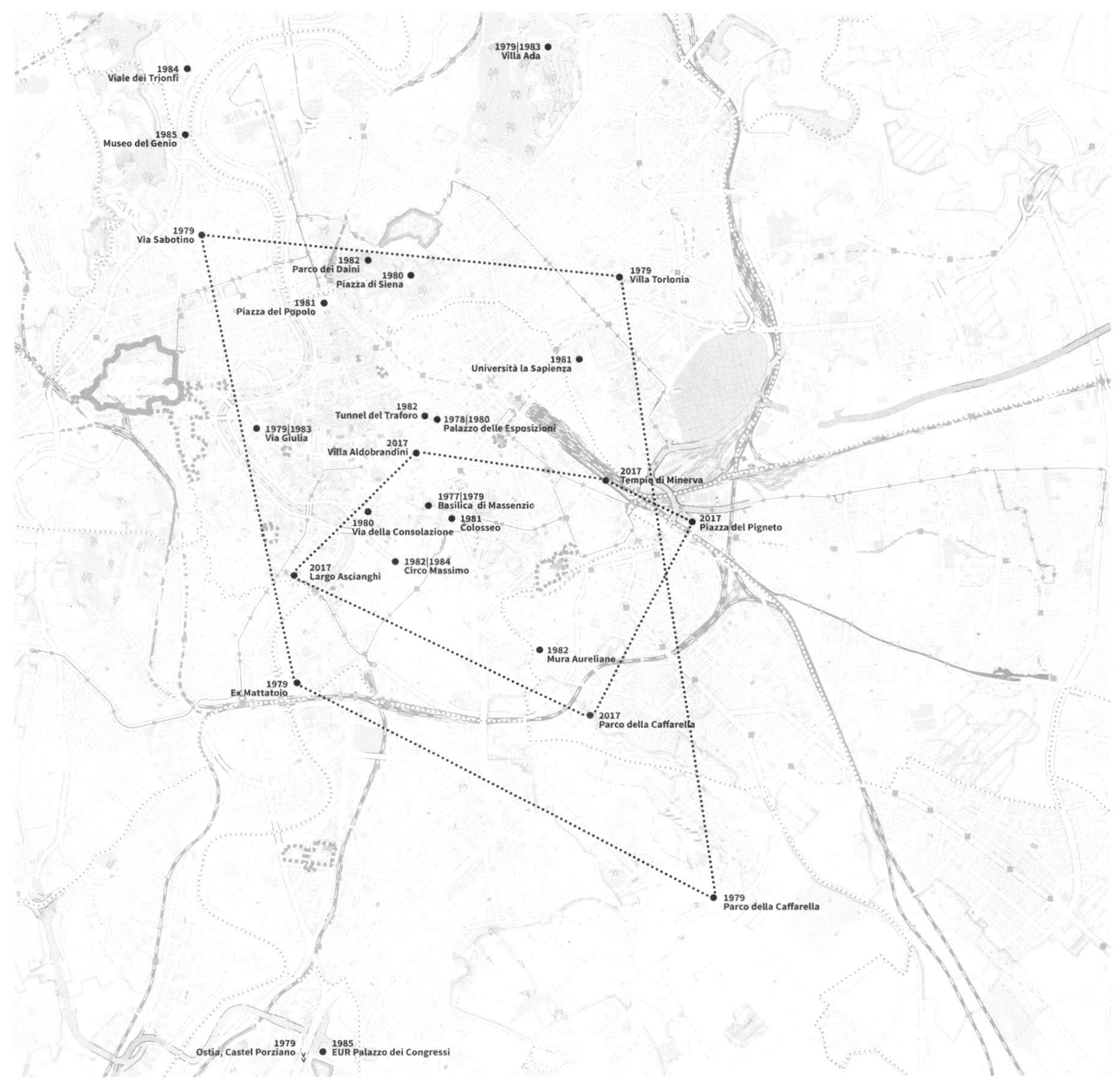

Map of the "Estate Romana" and "Parco Centrale" 1979/2017, Federica Fava, 2017. © Courtesy of Fondazione MAXXI

both by building a partial replica of Purini's Teatrino Scientifico for the 2017 summer events at MAXXI, and also through the production of the projects displayed in the DDP in Seoul. The curatorial team (from the MAXXI, the people from the City of Rome, our consultants) has chosen five "new" poles for the new Parco Centrale and has asked the five teams involved to design five "ephemeral" museums for the sites.

This leads directly to the third topic, which we can synthesize as the presence and role of the temporary (the "ephemeral") in contemporary architecture. Many reasons seem to make this approach quite appropriate to our times, and some of them deserve to be mentioned. First of all, there is the appeal of something we could call an "ecology of space." From many angles and through many studies we have learned how to develop alternative tactics for reaching architectural goals: "recycling," "re-using," "sharing," and "inhabiting spaces temporarily" are only some of the keywords in architectural discourse today.

The idea of the temporary fits perfectly in this picture, and it offers cities another option in the attempt to improve the quality of life and space for communities. Another context where temporary architecture has become an absolute protagonist is the museum. Following (and enfolding) a tradition that once belonged only to the garden of the Museum of Modern Art in New York and a few other spaces for vernacular replicas, architects are now more and more frequently asked to design specific structures for outdoor and indoor spaces in museums. It is an interesting phenomenon, with implications we don't have the time to discuss here, but it is also an important part of our discussion. An ephemeral project built in the context of a museum project is both a device to bring the city into the museum space and a device to expand the museum out into the city, which means stating the role of art as an agent of urban life, exactly as in the case of Estate Romana. To close the circle, for the Seoul Biennale the City of Rome proposes five projects which aim to support the most rooted aspects of the cultural industry of the city: cinema, theater, media, dance, opera and music, poetry and publishing. Here, temporary architecture is intended as a device to fuel and revive permanent resources, through the regeneration of abandoned spaces (the five theaters) and through the power of architectural expression.

San Diego / Tijuana
→ Go to Tijuana / San Diego, p.119

San Francisco
At Home Together

Neeraj Bhatia, Antje Steinmuller, Urban Works Agency

"The only indispensable material factor in the generation of power is the living together of people. Only where men live so close together that the potentialities of action are always present can power remain with them."
—Hannah Arendt, *The Human Condition*

In recent years, communal living in San Francisco has gained widespread attention for its potential to address the affordability crisis in this highly desirable location. While media accounts of this domestic typology typically describe it for its economic efficiency—incorporating it into simplistic narratives about gentrification and rising rents—this "necessity-oriented" explanation of communal residences misses the breadth of motivations and manifestations of intentional communities, from sociopolitical values to professional networking and lifestyle affinities. The notion of living together is not new to San Francisco. In fact, during the 1960s, San Francisco became a critical hub for the development of communes. The commune acted as a space for experimenting—on alternative politics,

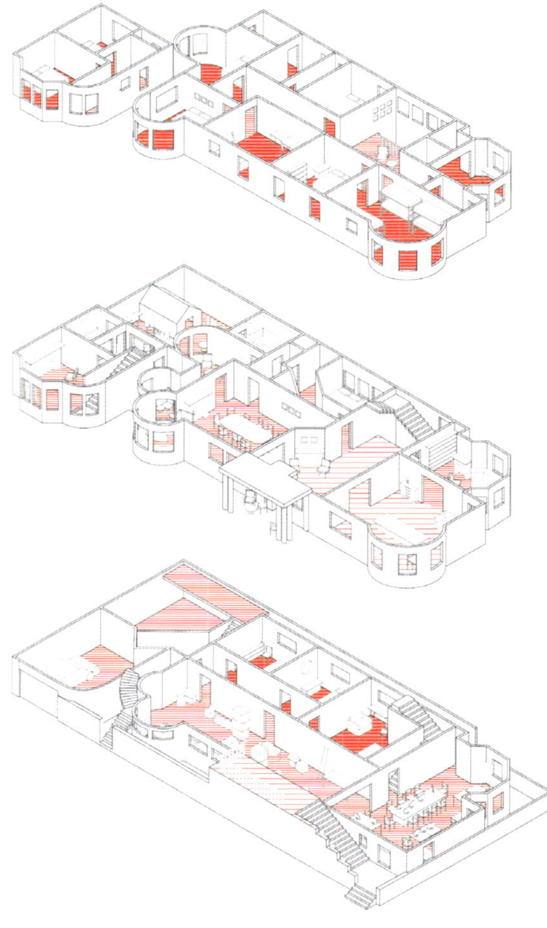

Spatial Typologies of Communal Living: EDWARDIAN DREAMS - A Cultural Hub © drawing by The Urban Works Agency / California College of the Arts

lifestyles, and attempting to go beyond the nuclear family. These spaces sought to more precisely curate a way of living that existed outside of the system. Against this backdrop, which has shaped the city, communal living is once again having a resurgence. Within a culture of the declining significance of the nuclear family, communal living has offered meaningful social units and the establishment of culture, values, community, and support. Not only has living together embraced a larger range of users, through sharing resources, these spaces inherently build a commons and offer a higher quality of social life. In parallel, contemporary modes of communal living have expanded from communes to include new experiments in co-living, hacker hostels and time-shared spaces among others. Several of these are tied to the rise of the sharing economy, which also emerged in San Francisco.

Peer-to-peer software experimentation has created an opportunity to effectively reorganize the city's resources and space, including housing. Reconsidering how we live, these platforms have effectively tapped into the transience of new forms of domestic life.

In the complex context of the resurgence of communal living, and against the backdrop of the well-known communes that shaped the image of San Francisco in the 1960s and 1970s, *At Home Together* analyzes the social and spatial typologies of contemporary co-living conditions—from the intentional to the unintentional—revealing how these domestic typologies leverage their hold on scarce urban space while shaping broader communities. Analyzing these domestic spaces through their spatial and social types as well as their political ideologies, the research aims to identify inherent patterns within the shifting

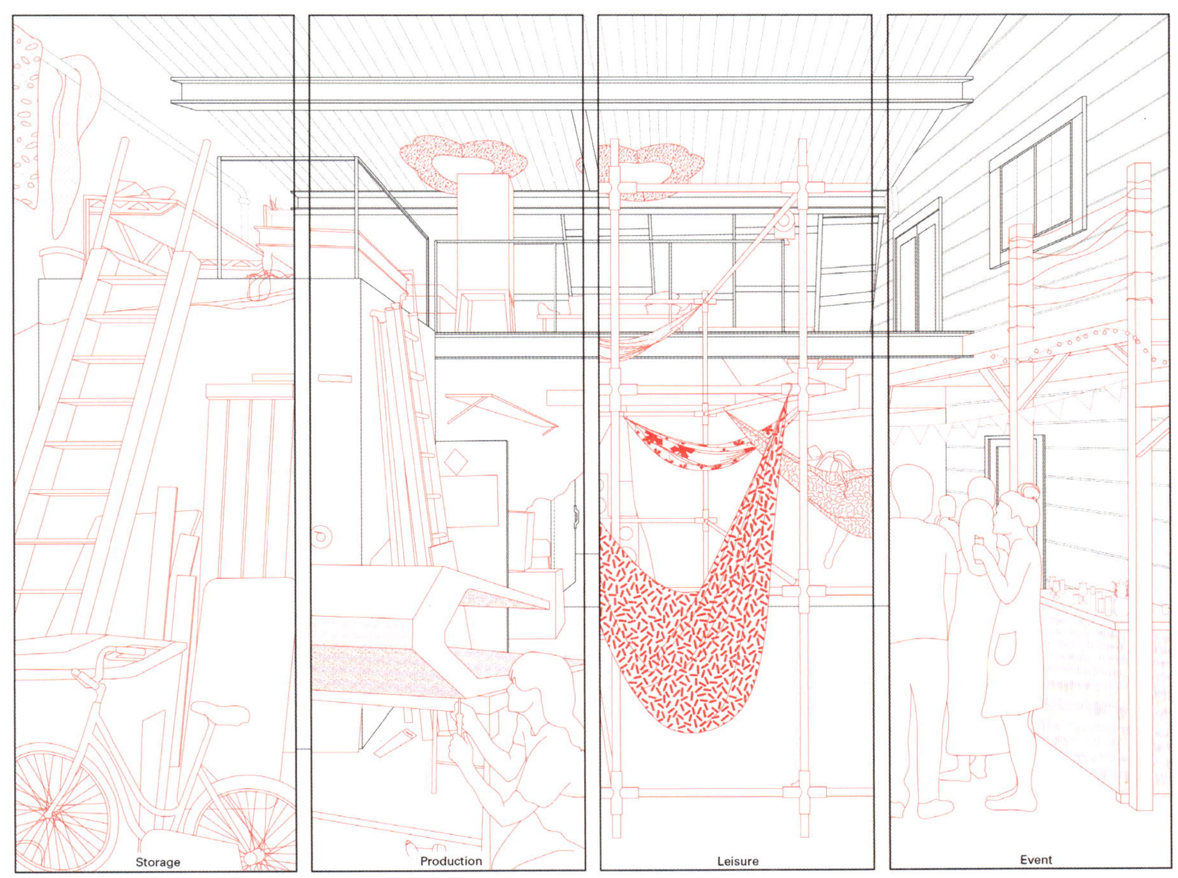

Typologies of Space Appropriation: THE ARTIST'S LABORATORY - A Markers' Warehome
© drawing by The Urban Works Agency / California College of the Arts

conceptions of the public and private spheres as they map themselves onto the hierarchical frameworks of today's urban environment. We recognize that living together is not easy; it requires compromise, negotiation, inconvenience, and patience. More importantly, it requires architectural design to mediate our lifestyles, scales of sharing, and uses over time. How we live together and how we gain privacy is the core of how our politics are shaped. *At Home Together* positions itself as a producer of concrete knowledge on how collective uses and spaces are shaped for reappropriation and interpretation.

The breadth of co-living experiments in San Francisco defies simple notions of what constitutes communal living today. Within the context of a housing crisis, contemporary communal living experiments offer a range of spaces, from affordable housing (necessity oriented) to spaces of alterity (politically oriented). Our contention is that no matter the motivations for living together, these spaces offer the potential for communities to more freely express how they want to live. Uncovering today's hidden communal experiments provides insight into the role of the domestic realm in relation to political participation, pluralism, and the conception of the public sphere in cities today. While several of these existing spatial typologies were originally designed for other purposes—typically to house a nuclear family—we argue that projective design can offer a possibility to more accurately reflect who we are today, and thereby how we can live. The spatial typologies—both existing and projective—frame the tension between the individual and the collective, the formal and the informal, high-tech and low-tech, between urban hardware and soft forms of reappropriation. While the home is emblematic of a private world, we ask how we can live together in one of our most intimate environments.

São Paulo
Food Circuit in São Paulo
Denise Xavier de Mendonça
Anderson Kazuo Nakano
Antonio Rodriges Netto

The Urban Food Question

In an increasingly urbanized world, more and more people meet their basic needs in cities, especially in such megacities as the metropolis and the municipality of São Paulo, with twenty-one and twelve million inhabitants, respectively.

Along with reliable access to safe drinking water, access to adequate and nutritious food in sufficient quantity is one of the most basic human needs that everyone has to satisfy in order to ensure survival.

Large cities have food circuits that connect production, storage, distribution, commercialization, consumption, and final disposal of the solid waste generated. The immense demand for food in such large cities as São Paulo means that these circuits must reach far distant places. In the face of this reality, the inhabitants of large cities are increasingly alienated from the origins of the foods they eat daily.

Aside from the sanitary problems of food, which are monitored and controlled by government agencies, there is widespread ignorance of the positive and negative effects that food can have on the human body. This creates a serious situation of food and nutritional insecurity that affects all social groups inhabiting the municipality of São Paulo, especially the poorest.

Along with other aspects of urban life (such as stress and sedentary lifestyles), food and nutritional alienation and insecurity, as well as excessive consumption of processed foods, are some of the causes of excess weight and obesity among teenagers and adults. In the city of São Paulo in 2012, approximately 17.5% of the twelve-to-eighteen-year-olds were overweight, and 5.5% were obese. Among adults over eighteen years of age, 52% were overweight, and 18% were obese.

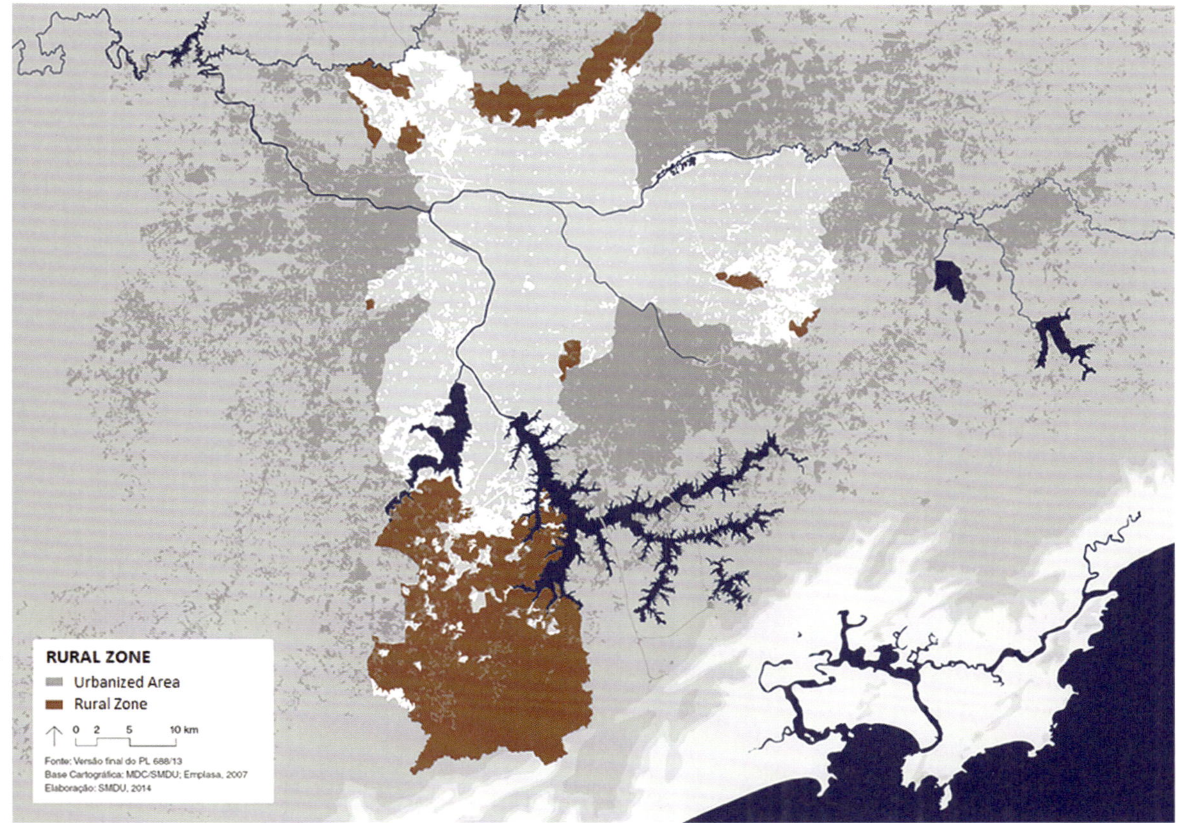

Rural Zone defined by the Strategic Master Plan of São Paulo Municipality. © Architect Ivan Alves Pereira

Long and Centralized Food Circuits Operated by Private Companies

In the city of São Paulo, the permit holders of the Company of General Shops and Warehouses of São Paulo (CGSWSP), the main food supplier for the city, sell 283,000 tons of assorted fruits and vegetables, flowers, fish, garlic, potatoes, onions, dried coconut, and eggs.

These products come from 1,500 municipalities located in twenty-two Brazilian states (or provinces), as well as from nineteen foreign countries. The centralized food supply operated by the CGSWSP does not extend access to natural, healthy foods (fruits and vegetables produced without pesticides) to the more peripheral neighborhoods of the city, which are inhabited mostly by low-income populations. Most people in these neighborhoods buy their food in supermarkets and hypermarkets without an alternative place to get natural and healthy food at more afford-able prices. In this way, they consume excessively processed foods and stop consuming the daily amount of fruits and vegetables that is necessary for the prevention of disease.

Short and Decentralized Food Circuits Conducted by Civil Society

Faced with the food and nutritional insecurity that marks contemporary urban life, members of São Paulo's civil society have come together to plant communal food gardens in squares, parks, schools, cultural centers, and on idle land, among other types of urban spaces.

Many residents organize groups to make collective purchases of natural and healthy food directly from local agricultural producers. These social organizations promote urban agriculture with the participation of low-income residents who live in peripheral neighborhoods.

Company of General Shops and Warehouses of São Paulo (CGSWSP). © Divulgação / CEAGESP

Short and Decentralized Food Circuits Proposed by the Municipal Government

In line with the contemporary search for greater food and nutritional security, the Strategic Master Plan of the Municipality of São Paulo, approved in 2014, defined rural areas with the objective of increasing local production and consumption of natural and healthy foods. The municipality's efforts to carry out this strategic plan are particularly important in the areas of environmental interest and of conservation and recovery of water resources.

The other objective is to contain the peripheral urban expansion that is advancing into rural areas. This kind of expansion is based mainly on the construction of low-income housing in precarious and informal urban settlements.

After the reinstitution of rural areas, the municipal government of São Paulo proposed a program aimed at strengthening the articulation between places dedicated to the production, storage, distribution, and consumption of agricultural produce. In 2016, Bloomberg Philanthropies awarded a US$5 million award to the São Paulo city government to support the implementation of this program.

These short and decentralized food circuits aim to include: 400 agricultural producers; training institutions, and technical assistance to agricultural producers; 1 storage and distribution center maintained by the municipal government; 2,500 municipal schools that serve 2 million meals monthly; 32 municipal markets; 880 street markets; 21 low-cost public restaurants; 1 composting plant, with 27 more proposed.

Sejong
Zero-Energy Smart City Development
National Agency for Administrative City Construction

With the Paris Agreement on climate change, the looming Fourth Industrial Revolution, and other changes in the background, discourse on urban planning is changing rapidly. Zero-energy goals and the smart city, for example, are immediate challenges faced by urban planners.

"Happy City[6] Zero-Energy Town (5-1 Community Zone[7])" is an environmentally sustain-

6. "Happy City" is a nickname for Sejong City. The city government seems to have adopted the name for an obvious reason: the word "happy." However, the nickname is also an acronym for "administrative city" in Korean, which was the working name before Sejong City was formally incorporated on July 1, 2012 (translator's note, hereafter t.n.).
7. A "community zone" or *saenghwalgwon* (literally a "biotope") in Korean, is bureaucratic, urban planning jargon. The use of this term reflects policy makers' desire for a departure from traditional urban planning and putting into practice some of the more recent, ongoing discussions regarding the

able urban model in which energy consumed is equal to energy produced. This equilibrium can be achieved through a synergetic relationship between new and renewable energy technologies on one hand, and information and communication technologies (ICT), such as smart grids, on the other.

In a net zero-energy city, the energy needed for buildings—for heating, air-conditioning, hot water, ventilation, and lighting, for example—is supplied by new and renewable energy produced locally. At the same time, the city energy grid is connected to an external grid. Any surplus energy produced is absorbed by the external grid while any shortage is supplemented by it. The idea is to make the net give and take of the energy a zero at the end of each year.

The first task for achieving this goal is to achieve the minimization of energy consumption and maximization of energy production and to have such a system built into urban facilities. This requires a new paradigm in zoning: allowing the exchange of surplus energies between internal and external energy grids.

More specifically, in 5-1 Community Zones, urban energy consumption will be minimized through efficient land use. For example, a "wind path" will be created using the "valley wind": this will lower urban temperature and minimize surface radiation. In order to maximize renewable energy through architecture, solar energy and geothermal heat (heat pump) will be tapped. Energy production will also be maximized: "energy furniture" will be installed throughout the site, and a section of the community zone will be dedicated to showcasing buildings that utilize special materials, or building-integrated photovoltaics (BIPVs).

In terms of energy management, 5-1 will utilize tools such as Building Energy Management System (BEMS), smart grids, and Energy Storage Systems (ESS) for efficient and systematic management. The 5-1 site as a whole

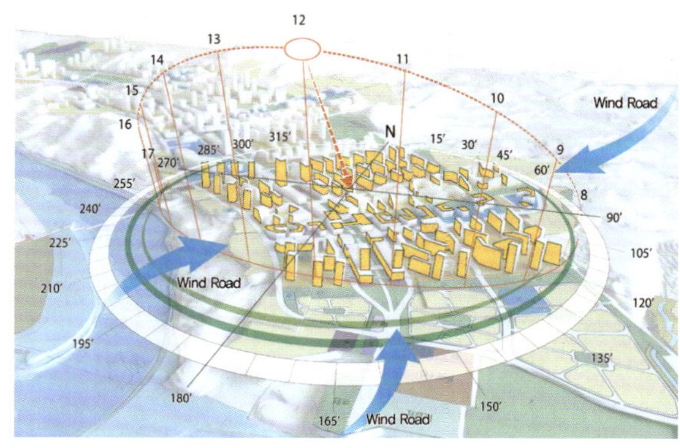

Building Layout Plan Taking Sunlight and Wind Direction into Consideration.

will save energy, and it will be able to manage energy more efficiently and systematically by the hour, by the day, and by the season, with information on energy usage patterns provided by the information and communication technologies, which will be built into many of the facilities at the site.

Institutions
The National Agency for Administrative City Construction (NAACC) is the government agency responsible for the construction of the "administrative city," now called Sejong City. Launched in 2006, the agency has been responsible for planning, managing, and attracting investment for the construction of Sejong, an integrated city with a concentration of government administrative buildings. The city was newly developed specifically to relocate a large segment of the Korean national government, the offices of which were traditionally concentrated in Seoul and its environs. The goal of the government relocation was a nationwide "balanced development" and a reduction of overpopulation in the larger metropolitan Seoul area. NAACC is proud of the historical mission it has been appointed to carry out, and we are doing our utmost to make sure that the new city becomes "a global benchmark city that everyone wishes to live in."

Korea Land and Housing Corporation
Korea Land and Housing Corporation is a public corporation established to promote the improvement of housing and the efficient use of national land. Its duties include the acqui-

environment and urbanism. More specifically, it refers to what might more ordinarily be called an "integrated" zone or city, where residents may enjoy commercial, residential, and public service amenities in an integrated way, and where people can work and live in the same place. While there are many "community zones" designated as such in Sejong City, "5-1 Community Zone" is special: at the end of 2016, it was selected as the first pilot project site for the Zero-Energy Town initiative. Construction is expected to be completed by 2030 (t.n.).

sition, development, banking, and supply of land; urban development and maintenance; and the construction, supply, and management of housing. By supplying 2.6 million units of public housing, the corporation has contributed to securing housing stability for the working poor. In addition, by developing new cities around the nation, it has developed land and expanded social overhead capital such as roads and schools, and thus contributed to the growth of the national economy. The corporation has undertaken the construction of the administrative city. As such, it exerts efforts to make sure that the new city will be representative of innovative urban planning, not only in Korea, but also globally.

Seoul
Sectioning Seoul

Sora Kim
Seoul Metropolitan Government

Seoul is a megacity that is currently home to one-fifth of South Korea's population. Historically, it has gone through periods of expansion and growth despite the geographic constraints intrinsic to it; relative to the size of the city population, available land for urban development in Seoul is extremely limited.[8] Modern urban planning regimes began to be introduced in Seoul beginning in the 1960s, a period in which the nation's full-fledged industrialization began. It was an urban planning regime that worked well historically for developing modern Western cities. In Seoul, however, where much of the terrain is mountainous, what worked well in flat Western cities was applied haphazardly; it was a plan steeped in a vision of urban planning that focused mainly on creating as much floor space as possible. The outcome is a massive structure of layered levels—at various heights and depths, above and below ground—that makes up today's Seoul. The layers may be characterized in four categories. The first is the underground layer. This layer has subterranean air-raid shelters,

8. Seoul is the capital of South Korea and its largest city. It is also one of the world's twenty-four megacities. Its land area accounts for only 0.57 percent of the total area south of the demilitarized zone, but its residents account for 19.4% of the nation's total population. A look at the city's zoning information shows that 38.7% of Seoul's land area is designated as a "green zone," meaning—for the most part—mountains. In other words, Seoul has a very small amount of land that can be developed. Seoul is compressed; it could not help but develop as a high-population-density city.

Sekwon Ahn, *Seoul Panorama Sewoon Sangga* (part), 2015 © Sekwon Ahn

passages, as well as subway tracks and other structures constructed deep below the bed of the Han River. The second is the above-ground layer developed to accommodate waves of population growth. It includes various policy-related and urban planning zones, high-density zones such as housing development zones (*taekji gaebal jigu*), land reallocation zones (*toji guhoek jeongni jigu*), and urban redevelopment zones (*jaegaebal jigu*). The third layer consists of elevated roads and high-rise buildings, the former constructed to accommodate the ever-increasing demand for faster transportation and thus the increasing vehicle traffic, while the latter, represented by countless "decks," may even occupy spaces above the ground-level traffic lanes. The fourth layer is the hilly areas, occupied by the urban poor who have been evicted from downtown areas and other urban flatlands.

These are the four layers that currently characterize Seoul and its cross-sectional structure. The layers are characterized by the fact that they are disconnected from one another and that the development or settlement of each layer was spearheaded by, or resulted from, the government urban planning regimes applied in a top-down manner during the era of industrialization and rapid economic growth. The different layers were developed to meet the changing demands of traffic, flood control, housing, national economic competitiveness, municipal and national identity as an advanced city and nation, and military readiness.[9] As such, the layers have created major

9. Urban zoning was first publicly promulgated for Seoul in 1936 by what was then the colonial government. Since that time, urban planning in Seoul has focused mainly on expanding planned urban zones (*dosi gyehoek guyeok*) and on accommodating the rapidly increasing population. Large-scale land reallocation, housing development, and road construction took place concurrently. By 1966, Seoul finally had a blueprint for a network of roads befitting a modern city. To deal with extreme automobile traffic congestion, interchanges and elevated roads were built. They were symbols of modern Western cities, and their implementation would contribute to realizing the image of Seoul as an "advanced" city. By the late 1990s, there were 120 elevated roads for car traffic, criss-crossing Seoul above the ground level. They were a symbol of economic growth and speed. The Cheonggye elevated road was built in the 1960s after the demolition of a sprawling slum along the Cheonggye stream. The stream was then covered up, and the elevated road was built. Yujin Sangga (Yujin shopping area) was also built after a similar process in the 1970s in Hongje-dong, another neighborhood in Seoul about five kilometers from the Cheonggye area. The lot on which Sewoon Sangga was built was originally an anti-air–attack evacuation facility built on public land by the Japanese. In the wake of the Korean War, war victims began to occupy the site. Later in the 1970s, the occupants were evicted, and due to the financial constraints of the city government, Sewoon Sangga, a landmark "high-rise" at the time, was built with private financing.

The first appearance of an underground public plaza in Seoul was a passage below the Gwanghwamun intersection. It was constructed to make sure that foot traffic did not interfere with the heavy flow of car traffic above ground. The decisive moment for expanding the underground layer of the city came in the wake of the 1968 infiltration of Seoul by armed

Seoul Mapping collage. © original map: Seungbum Kim, design: Junha Jeon, 05Studio

and minor peripheries and centers as well as public spaces and lives in which inequality, not equality, thrives.

Cross-Sections of Seoul: How They Divide the City into Peripheries and Centers

The elevated highway along the banks of the Han River makes casual access to the river difficult for people living in the neighborhoods nearby. The elevated walkway, on the other hand, cuts off pedestrian connections between neighborhoods on the ground level. Elevated roads and walkways create dark shadows, both literally and symbolically. The shadows and the noise from the elevated structures create peripheries within the living spaces of the urban population; they reduce the quality of public space. They lead to demarcation of social differences and entrenchment of social inequalities. Currently, the underground layer in Seoul is experiencing a loss of foot traffic. This is partly due to the fact that, in accordance with the national traffic control policy, many—if not all—urban traffic intersections now have pedestrian crossings; in the past there were almost none, which forced pedestrians to use the underground passages. An additional cause of the reduced underground traffic may be found in the lack of organically designed, seamless entries into the underground from ground level. These underground spaces are becoming a cause for worry about night-time crime for those who use them after hours. In their original design, they were built with a horizontal view of the city, not a vertical view; the connections between spaces above and below are counter-intuitive, and the entrances are

North Korean guerrillas. The incident set off a wave of legislative and other reactions. The fortification of the city began in earnest. Basements became mandatory, as they would be used as air-raid shelters in case of emergency. Furthermore, the subway lines that connected Seoul with its outer metropolitan areas would now be built below the riverbed of the Han River. This created multiple layers of underground space in Seoul. Many of the hilly neighborhoods in Seoul are located near the historical city wall. During the Joseon period, the wall had a military function, while also serving as a place for contemplation. During the colonial period, mud hut villages began forming in various areas near the wall. In more recent history, war and disaster victims, and those who were forcibly evicted from urban flatlands—the redevelopment areas—began settling down in these areas; with the absence of basic urban infrastructure or public amenities, these hillside areas quickly became slums. Because of the steep grade in these neighborhoods, streets are narrow and winding, which led to them being excluded from urban redevelopment. Although these neighborhoods are neither military facilities nor otherwise restricted, they are seldom visited by outsiders because the steep grade makes access to the area by the general public difficult.

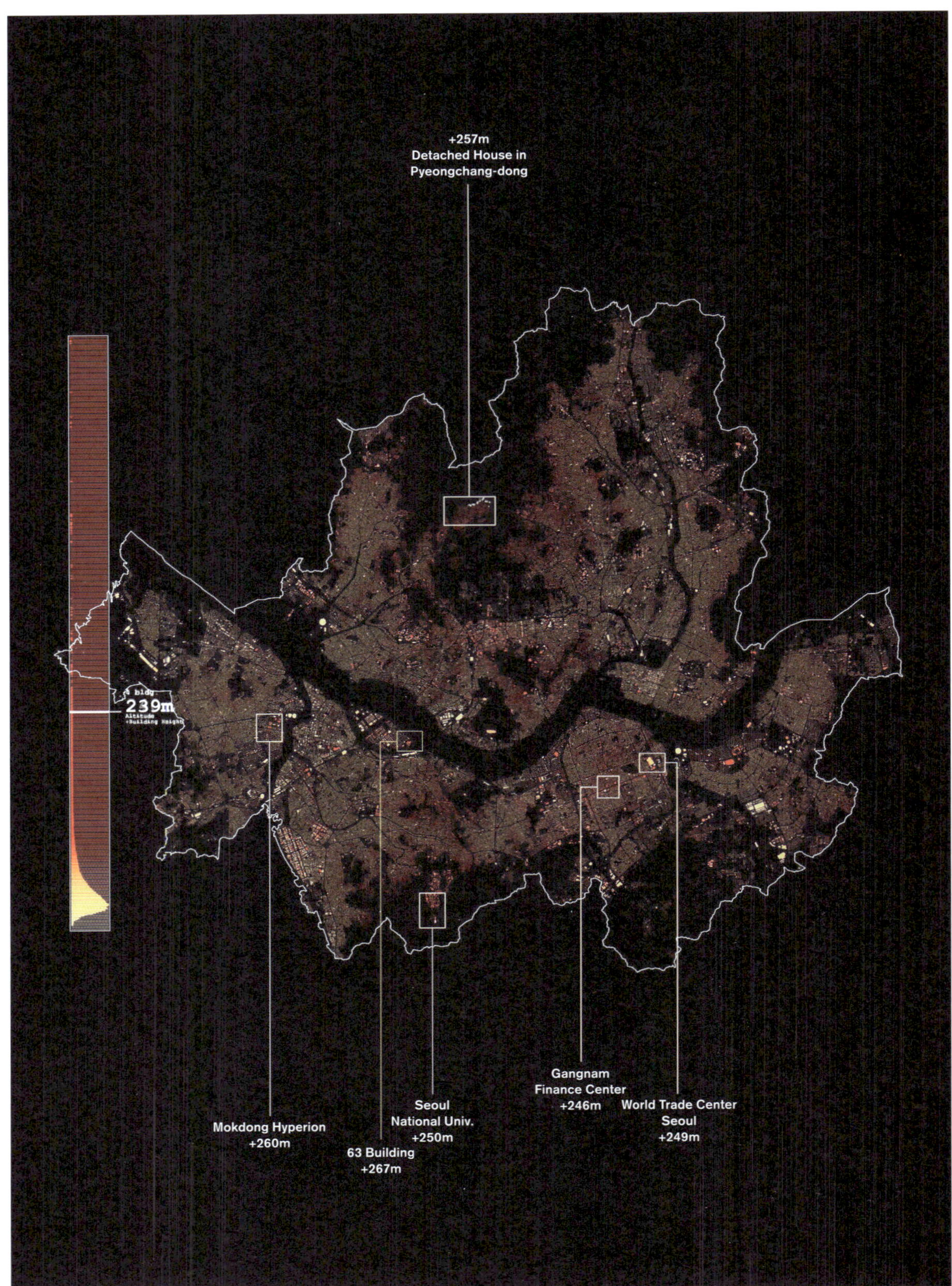

Comparison of sea level altitude in Seoul buildings. *Seoul Scanner*, Video © Seungbum Kim

unwelcoming. Considering the size of the vast underground spaces, there is a lack of variety of uses. Clearly, these factors contribute to the widening gap between the underground and aboveground layers.

Where the altitude makes it not too cost-prohibitive, the hillside urban areas have all but disappeared from public view due to the redevelopment of former shantytown areas and the construction of ever more high-rise buildings. Hills have disappeared from view, blocked by skyscrapers soaring into heights much greater than the hills. In these newly redeveloped hillside neighborhoods, one cannot appreciate the unique sensual experience of the hillside neighborhoods they replaced. In the waves of urban redevelopment, hillside neighborhoods have been pushed out from the urban center; the "hillside" now represents the periphery, the "other." As for hillside neighborhoods at higher altitudes, where redevelopment plans have been suspended due to topographical restraints, residents cannot enjoy many of the public services that most other citizens enjoy, even though the radial distance of their neighborhood to the city centers is the same as some of the other neighborhoods. Direct bus routes and train lines are not available to visit markets, hospitals, libraries, senior citizen centers, or community centers. Thus while residents in such neighborhoods are not far from urban centers in terms of radial distance, the degree of their social alienation and psychological isolation is equal to that of residents on the outskirts of Seoul.

A Change of Direction in Seoul's Urban Planning Policies

By the 2000s, population growth in Seoul stabilized, and the demographic make-up began to change. Economic and social environments also changed greatly. An awareness that the status quo growth strategy was no longer valid began to arise. It signaled a need for a change, a need to turn away from the existing planning regime entrenched in master planning and authoritarian eviction practices. A new point of view was needed. The projects introduced in the exhibition show examples of "drop" solutions suggested from a sectional, rather than a horizontal, or planar, perspective of Seoul.

The elevated road near Seoul Station, a major transportation hub and historical landmark, had been scheduled to be demolished; however, under the new policy regime it was reborn as an automobile-free pedestrian park. The park now reconnects two sides of a neighborhood that had been divided by the railroad tracks running through it. Furthermore, the park rightfully returns the view of Namsan, Seoul's landmark mountain, back to the city's pedestrians. At one end of this park, named Seoullo (Seoul Avenue), there is an underground square called Yoonseul ("quietly rippling water surface reflecting the light from the moon or the sun"); there are also major and minor nodes that connect the pedestrians either from elevated space or ground level to nearby streets and into major buildings in the vicinity. These features of the park emphasize a sectional or cross-cut view of Seoul, not a view from a planar perspective.

Another project marking the policy turnaround in Seoul is the project currently on going at Sewoon Sangga, a consumer electronics Mecca during its heyday in the 1970s and 1980s. The new "aerial" pedestrian passage will return the view of Jongmyo, the Royal Ancestral Shrine, and Namsan to pedestrians. The passage also functions as a street that connects Sewoon Sangga to surrounding areas that are slated for redevelopment. This municipal project will function as an engine for urban renewal in the Sewoon Sangga area; for example, the decades-old inner-city manufacturing industry, which has been experiencing a severe decline, will now be connected to new industries emerging in the city.

A new underground plaza slated to be built on the site of the former National Tax Service Annex building will be connected to the Deoksu Palace underground pedestrian passage, which in turn is connected to the subways and the underground Citizens Hall across the street at City Hall. The structure protruding above ground will be constructed in line with the height of the historic palace's stone wall. The purpose of these attempts to seamlessly connect the various under- and above-ground spaces—at some point in the near future the new underground plaza near the palace, the City Hall underground facilities, the Eulji-ro underground passages, the streets above ground, and the Sewoon Sangga "skywalk" will all connect in a seamless network—is to find new utility from partial improvements of the vast areas of urban underground spaces already in existence.

Various hillside villages that have been alienated from enjoying the convenience and benefits of urban living are now attempting to shed marginalization through public-private collaboration programs, in which local residents participate actively, and that work with their location-specific characteristics. Haeng-chon is one such neighborhood. Because of its hilly location, it boasts an abundance of sunlight; the residents enjoy rooftops as if they were flatlands. Utilizing this topography-specific feature of the village, the residents operate an urban-farming co-op. As in the case of this village, new experiments are being carried out where residents in hillside villages self-provide necessary daily services on a small scale through resident associations and village co-ops.

Seoul Renewal Using a Cross-Sectional Approach: New Utility for Urban Layers

The problem of the separation of center and periphery in the city is the result of the top-down, government-led, master plan approach of the past, which was steeped in the flat, area–focused perspective of urban planning. Seoul is now pursuing a new paradigm for urban renewal that focuses on a cross-sectional view of the city, or on how to organically connect the various levels of the city below and above ground. The goal of the new paradigm is to improve the physical connectivity of neighborhoods that have been divided, to improve accessibility between the layers of the city, and to find new utility for spaces that have been underutilized. The future of Seoul, as shown by the new approach, is as a city in which urban planning is done with the topography and cross-sectional view of the city in mind, not with an exclusively horizontal view. Rather than taking the approach of viewing a whole block of an urban area as a single plane, urban planning will take a "drop" method approach, in which a key location or area is identified in order to provide a solution for the larger, affected area; rather than enforcing top-down, government-initiated programs, urban planning will work with local residents who will exercise autonomy in planning their own domains of living.

**Seongbuk Cultural Foundation
(Young Art Space)
Co-op Art Plug**

Since the beginning of the nineteenth century, many artists, writers, and other cultural notables in Korea have made their home in the Seongbuk-dong area, making it a center of artistic activities. Today the tradition continues. A quick glance at the names of famous houses and institutions tells the neighborhood's storied history: Seongrakwon, Suyeon-sanbang, Simwujang, Gansong Museum, the Furniture Museum, and Gilsangsa. In short, the area is a treasure trove of important historical resources on architecture, literature, art, and culture that overlap modern and contemporary periods in Korea. In more recent years, a variety of artistic and cultural spaces have been popping up along the streets in what were before strictly residential areas. The new spaces thus emerging in the neighborhood form an archipelago of art galleries, museums, artists' studios, theatre spaces, craft workshops, workshops, gallery-cafes, and architects' offices. Artists, writers, actors, performers, musicians, film professionals, and architects are active in the area. They have built a wide-ranging network with local residents and business owners.

Seongbuk Art Commons is an imaginary entity; it is an ideal art community where artists and local residents live in harmony based on an economy of sharing. This exhibition presents various imaginary and real examples of *Seongbuk Art Commons*. In its imaginary state, the commons is a very small city situated in the hilly Seongbuk-gu, Seoul. In real life, through various artistic and cultural spaces and activities in Seongbuk-gu, artists and local residents have been connecting with each other in important ways. They have sought to share common public values and to safeguard them. In an effort to meet this goal, a number of different networks are in operation. They include Round Table on Share Seongbuk, Seongbuk Visual Arts Network, Art Plug Co-op, Citizens for Seongbuk Samsun Art Village, and From Eight. Facilitators of these organizations have been working and coordinating with the local *gu* (district) office and the Seongbuk Cultural Foundation to implement a variety of community-based programs. *Seoungbuk Art Commons* is one such program; other programs/events include the annual Seongbuk Global Food Festival and A Neighborhood Artist. There was also the Save the Trees in Seongbuk-dong campaign in 2016. This campaign started when plans to cut two large old trees in the name of improving traffic were set without consulting the community. The residents found out before the trees were completely uprooted and removed. They protested and it was eventually decided that the trees would stand where they are; their tops still cut off, the *gu* office will take measures to make sure that the trees survive and grow new branches. This was not only a sweet

victory for local residents, but also a symbolic moment. It shows how art and aesthetic resistance can be translated directly into social practice and into realizing public value. This victory was made possible by the community network, an artistic ecosystem that *Seongbuk Art Commons* aims to cultivate. Looking ahead, there are plans to transform various vacant properties and idle facilities in the area into public art spaces. The former water supply "booster station" in the Seongbuk area and the former headquarters belonging to Haedong Landscape, a private company, were recently brought to public attention.

The exhibition features flowerpots. They symbolize nature and people. Seongbuk-dong is close to nature, as characterized by the mountainous terrain and waterways. Historically, a large stream flowed down the middle of the neighborhood between two mountain ranges, and the entire neighborhood is surrounded by mountains and by the ancient city wall. In terms of people, the neighborhood population has always been diverse, and the countless small streets and alleyways have made co-existence intimate. Some people grow potted plants or flowers outside their rooms and houses, casually breaking down

KANG Ui-seok, *Save the Trees in Seongbuk-dong*, 2016, Video.

the barriers between private and public spaces and generating solidarity between the two spaces. Along with the flowerpots, the three-dimensional structures connected to the acrylic chamber show the map of *Seongbuk Art Commons*, project videos, and other archive materials. Together, they represent a compressed version of *Seongbuk Art Commons*, its geographical connectivity in real life. The exhibition is also an extension of *2017 Seongbuk Art Commons*, an annual event. There will be exhibitions, performances, and other projects taking place at thirty-odd venues around the neighborhood. The venues include spaces with geographical and/or historical significance, contemporary art spaces, vacant lots or buildings, and neighborhood streets. Participants and visitors will be able to witness firsthand *Seongbuk Art Commons* as it actually is. It is a neighborhood art community founded on the principles of respecting nature and life, one that aspires to live and work in harmony with other artists, local business owners, and the residents. The hope is that the example of *Seongbuk Art Commons* will inspire other contemporary cities to imagine alternative models of community.

**SH Corporation
Seoul Housing and Community Movements 1:
Towards Open Communities**

Jieun Kim (Seoul Housing and
Communities Corporation)
Tae Jin Lee
Gyeong Oh Chung (05Studio)

Dong-nae (neighborhood) is a word that is familiar yet strange in contemporary Seoul. The warm connotation of a *dong-nae* is inevitably associated images of small- or moderate-scale houses huddled together. However, today, the more familiar scene of a *dong-nae* is an apartment complex of high-rises, usually with the corporate logo of the construction company visible from miles away. These apartment buildings come complete with standardized living quarters, plenty of underground parking spaces connected directly to one's apartment door and elevator, playgrounds for children, and exclusive "community centers" for the

residents. Surrounded by these amenities, residents would wonder how they ever lived in low-rise houses. Somewhere in the hushed corners of old, low-rise neighborhoods, one would inevitably find, on any given day, a desire for one of these high-rise apartments hovering above.

Ten years ago, redevelopment fever completely swept through low-rise residential areas in Seoul. People were anxious that they would be left behind, in every sense of the word, and everyone jumped onto the redevelopment bandwagon. The code name for the fever was "Newtown," examples of which were consequently built everywhere. However, the fever began to die down, symbolically marked in January 2009 by the death of six people in Yongsan during a violent clash between police and tenants who faced eviction. By then, one-third of all residential areas in Seoul were designated as "pre-development" zones. As of the current date, out of the 683 pre-development zones that had been designated, 356 decided not to go ahead with their plans. Currently, local residents and city decision-makers are together seeking new solutions to transform old low-rise residential areas into attractive neighborhoods.

This exhibition proposes that through a new private-public approach, low-rise areas in Seoul can be transformed into "open complexes." An open complex is a residential regeneration model. Its aim is to make old residential areas into attractive urban neighborhoods. Each open complex has its own parking lot, a day care center, a senior citizens center, a small library, and lockers for storing parcel deliveries. Rejecting exclusivity and espousing the values of openness and a community, it is a residential complex with the amenities of the high-rise apartment complex.

The basic unit of an open complex is approximately 200 meters in radius. This is so that anyone, in particular children and the elderly, can reach the amenities of the complex within ten minutes' walk. The size is also intended to encourage busy residents to take interest and participate in small and large changes in and around their homes on their way to and from work.

Seoul Housing and Communities Corpora-

Seoul Neighborhood, 2017. Photo source: *Seoul 2005 Urban Form and Landscape* (Seoul Metropolitan Government, 2006). © 05Studio

tion, in active cooperation with the municipal government, is participating in creating open complexes through innovative projects. One such project is developing public properties, such as dilapidated community centers or public parking lots, into multi-use complexes. Such a complex would have, for example, parking facilities on the underground level, amenities for the community on the lower levels, and public housing on the upper levels. Providing communal housing in cooperation with "social enterprises" is also an important means of providing for optimal housing and communal activities. Owners of old houses in a neighborhood may come together to build a small-scale apartment building, expanding narrow streets and securing spaces for necessary community facilities. Providing support for such projects is a new role demanded of the public sector. The projects introduced in the exhibition are only a starting point for building open complexes. It is the beginning of a movement to build communities, to bring to life the meaning of *dong-nae* in Seoul, where it has become an unfamiliar concept over the years. The organizers of the exhibition invite the viewers to meet the future *dong-nae* in Seoul.

SH Corporation
Seoul Housing and Community Movements 2:
Landscripts for New Communities:
Seoul via Vienna

Haewon Shin
Mladen Jadric
Seoul Housing and Communities Corporation

"You never change things by fighting the existing reality. To change something, build a new model that makes the existing model obsolete."
—R. Buckminster Fuller

Landscripts for New Communities: Seoul via Vienna is a project that presents designs for twenty-two small neighborhoods inside the Hope Village (Sanggye-Village) in Seoul.

The visual presentation includes not only the designs, but also the project's guiding idea, which is explained through eight categories: topography, pad, road, way of life, design, environment, micro-economy, and community.

The program framework is based on a symbiosis of the two cities' best experiences, which demonstrate that affordable housing is a basic requirement and an essential ingredient of a just, inclusive, and sustainable city of tomorrow.

Eleven detailed approaches are shown in eight books; these demonstrate different strategic and rigorous design positions from the conceptual stage to a developed design proposal. They are based on an in-depth understanding and appreciation of design principles that apply to the selected category. The new neighborhoods demonstrate a deep respect

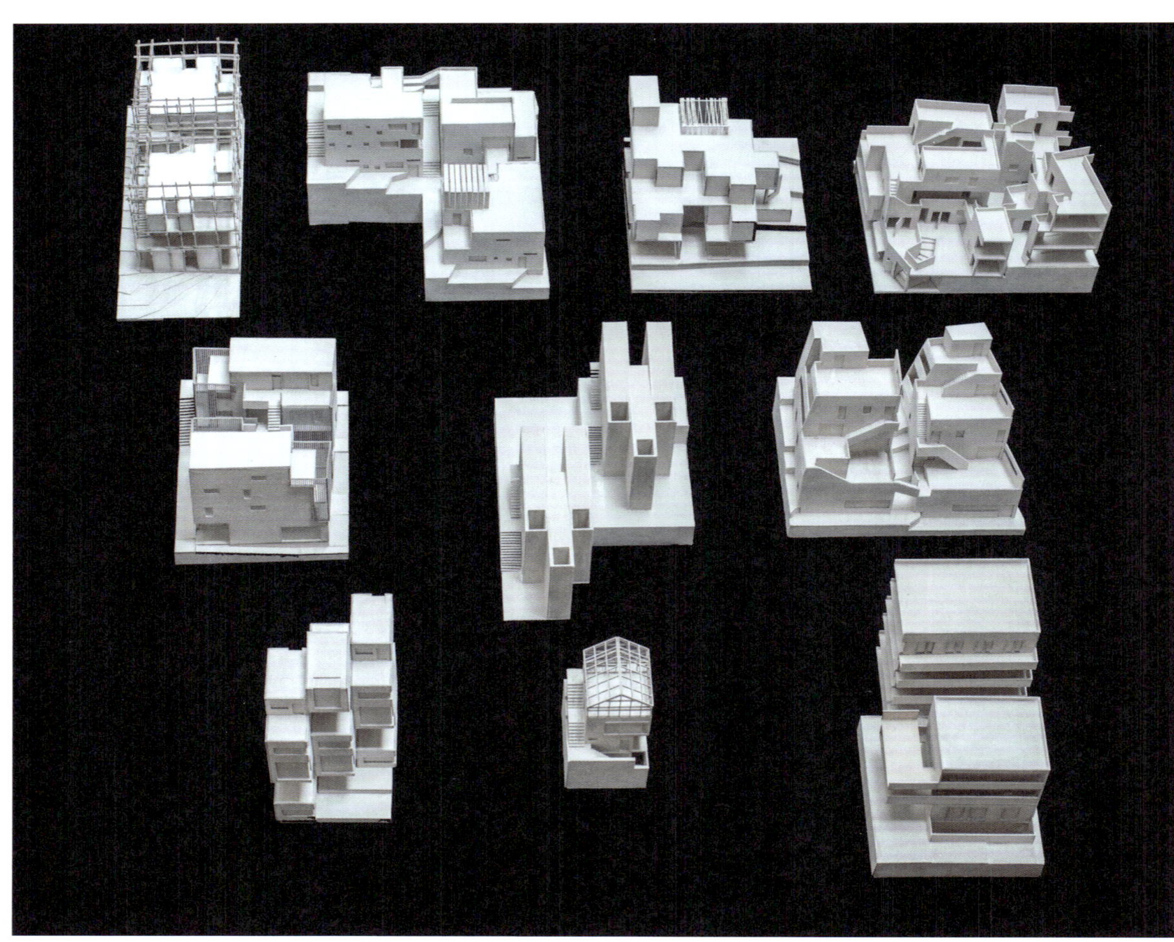

Low-rise high density Housing Typology. © Photo by Georg Mayer

for the local way of life including social, economic, and environmental responsibility.

Virtual visits through the high-density, low-rise neighborhoods show different layers of building and the related complex context of the contemporary urban conditions, which the City of Seoul could use as a pilot project for future housing models.

Topography

"Topography" refers to geographical characteristics that were formed ages ago. As all lands have distinct locations, their features are all different, but at the same time, all lands are closely connected to each other in all directions. Damaging the topography of one place causes a disconnect in other geographical locations, which is going against the law of nature. The Korean Peninsula has predominantly mountainous topography. Most of the flatlands of Korea are used as farmlands, since rice is a staple in the Korean diet; therefore, most Korean villages have been located on the hills. Since Korean houses are built on slopes, the construction must follow the topography of the land, and thus the entire village would accommodate itself to the topography.

Pad

"Pad" shows the history of the land as it was changed by humans to live on earth. Some pads were the first land that human beings settled upon; others were later created on top of the previous pads, forming an overlapping landscape of habitation. All pads are specific and definite signs of the human will to live on the land. Pads themselves are unique landscape alterations that were created not by nature but by humans; they are cultural landscapes. Most of the pads, particularly in the Korean landscape with its many hills, are small, so they cannot hold large buildings. As such, preserving those pads means protecting the cultural landscape of Korea.

Road

Western cities are usually located on flatlands. In order to divide the land and make efficient connections, the roads in new housing developments are paved first, so they are mostly straight lines. However, because most Korean houses are on hills, the houses must be built first; then the roads are paved in between the houses. Because of the hills, the roads cannot be straight lines, and the widths are all different. They are sometimes curving and wide or narrow and steep. These roads are not just used as passages, but as places for meeting, playing, and resting. Sometimes, a community can hold festivals or organize community work where all the people participate. Roads can be locations for strengthening solidarity and friendships. These are the reasons why roads are important public spaces in the memory of communities. Preserving these roads means conserving the history of Korean communities.

Way of Life

Preservation of living spaces must not be just a physical activity: sustainable communities must respect the way of life of native residents. Protecting their way of life means that we are preserving our history. Not only physical aspects that people have relied upon, but also people's way of life must be protected. For example, people must be allowed to continue cultivating their farmlands and managing their stores. The community spaces for people to gather must be preserved to make sure they will be able to stay in their places. Of course, the happiness of families in the communities must be ensured. Nevertheless, the way of life will change as new facilities come and affect the old ways, but this should not be hastened. We must be aware that not all structures are designed wholly by architects or construction companies.

Design

Quality of architectural design matters. It produces more value for tenants and promotes sustainable urban development. Residential architecture always mirrors the society for which it is made. Housing typologies and models reflect a successful integration of architectural design and ecology, economy and social sustainability. A synchronized design process improves design elements and the shapes of spaces on every scale: inside single apartments, inside buildings, and in entire

settlements. The objective of design is to address residents' needs, encourage interaction
among social classes, and promote innovation
and high-quality public and shared spaces.
Originality of architectural typologies is not an
expression of style, but of a new model of urban living. They challenge settled models and
promote variety in contemporary residential
architecture.

Environment

Mass migration into cities inflicts permanent
damage on the natural world within their
boundaries. Particularly affected are the outly-
ing metropolitan areas; thus, our focus here
is the preservation of the natural environment
and the creation of healthy neighborhoods.
In the conditions of extreme density typical in
newly built areas, the goal is to create an environmentally responsible lifestyle with a network of green areas and common spaces. The
design of "urban furniture" and "green rooms"
has to respond to technical and ecological criteria by taking into account the needs of different user groups. A further goal is to bring
about improvements in energy standards, and
in the use and production of renewable energy, as well as to minimize material flows and
emissions in the construction of residential
buildings.

Micro-Economy

The basic requirement of subsidized housing
is its financial viability for both developers and
users. Two strategies are in place:

a) First, the main purpose of a design process is to minimize the cost of construction
and building equipment, and consequently
to reduce the costs for end-users, including
tenancy terms.

b) Second, the purpose of the design process is to create spaces that promote existing
micro-economic networks and facilitate new
sources of income for tenants. Public funding
and well-organized vocational communities
greatly improve the rentability of subsidized
housing. In terms of comprehensive sustainability, smart design ensures a proper balance
of initial investment and follow-on maintenance costs.

Community

The planners are expected to design an infrastructure that enables socialization through
strategic planning of specific community
areas, both indoor and outdoor.

Every housing project contains sub-proj-
ects that promote social mixing—women's
emancipation, integration of disabled and
elderly people, immigrants' assimilation—and
provide educational and cultural content as a
principle of coexistence. In doing so, planners
demonstrate a high level of awareness of the
requirements for everyday life. Spatial organization and sequencing are primarily meant
to enable socialization and promote already
existing networks on every scale: among the
most immediate neighbors, within housing
blocks, and on streets across neighborhoods.
A proper organization of a housing unit will
create an identity by linking all the spaces "in
between." The goal is to motivate tenants to
actively and independently participate in community life because they wish to do so.

The City of Vienna has declared affordable
housing a basic requirement and an essential
ingredient of a just, inclusive, and sustainable
city. One of the key accomplishments is its
one-hundred-year tradition and experience in
building subsidized housing as well as in "soft"
renewal of the city. Vienna's experience could
be shared and established as an international model of synergy that takes into account
economic, environmental, architectural, and
social elements.

Shanghai
The Other Factory: Late-Industrial Organization and Form

H. Koon Wee
SKEW Collaborative

This research is a close investigation of the
process of industrialization in Shanghai in the
twentieth century. It reveals a particular history of—and potential for—Shanghai, by identifying the indirect effects of industrialization
in the context of a relentless form of urbanization that has been ubiquitous in China in
the last decade. This work would also begin
to describe the cycles of industrialization

and deindustrialization, in a global ecosystem of rust belts and collapsed economies, in relation to the rise of newly industrialized and urbanized nations. The by-product of the global manufacturing economy has led to the formation of unsuspecting and alienated consumers around the world, people whose lives are cross-subsidized by the poorer newly industrialized cities. In the city of Shanghai, the late-industrial and post-industrial built forms that would in turn become instantaneous building stock for the next invention of a city. The late-industrial forms and organization in Shanghai would suggest that the industrial typology is now highly unstable and evolving, with a stronger need for hybridity. Hence, there is a departure from Nikolaus Pevsner's factory typology and the modern treatment of a highly segregated system of industrial land use in cities. There is an emergence of a highly reflexive non-type that follows the conditions of rapid urbanization and structural changes in socio-economic realms. It is also important to extend Reyner Banham's critique of the aesthetics of the machine taking the place of the scientific and economic rationale in order to argue for a new form of aesthetics emerging in late-industrial Shanghai.

The new industrial organizational complex remains a legacy of Lewis Mumford's account of the mechanical clock and how urban time organizes the formation of industries and cities. These historically inseparable concepts of "cultural preparation" would have unexpected expressions in the cases of Shanghai. This is an inescapable organizational complex that governed cities in a particular period in history, but the liberal capitalization and urbanization processes in China are seeking to readjust the same industrial-consumerist space and time. One would also have to update Herbert Marcuse's critique of a totalitarian form of scientific rationale in advanced post-industrial societies. This "non-terroristic

Sedan Car Workshop in the Shanghai Auto Manufacturing Factory in the 1960s. © Image Courtesy of Zhongguo qiche wushinian, Shanghai Pictorial Publishing House

Reconstruction and Adaptive Reuse of Old Prefabricated Structures of the Chinese Academy of Sciences Laboratories designed by the Soviets during the Sino-Soviet Alliance Friendship Treaty in the 1950s. © Image courtesy of SKEW Collaborative

economic-technical coordination," which manipulates organization, industry, and productivity in the creation of a bureaucracy in the United States, would not have the same results in Socialist China.

The study of three sites of industrial organization and form corresponds with three dominant periods of industrialization in Shanghai, namely those of the Sino-Soviet Alliance, Cultural Revolution, and Open Door and Economic Reform. Key historical planning and socio-economic policies and strategies are included in the exhibition, including many diagrams, policies, maps, photographs, and other archival materials. There is also mapping and documentation of organizational networks formed by global and regional actors, such as the governmental research institutions, state agencies, private manufacturers, and other agencies.

Three key agencies are being studied under this research, following the organizational formation of each of them through time, and identifying the built forms across the city that corresponds to various formations of Chinese society. Such formations include technological change, education and labor improvements, urbanization, and many others. One of the key agencies at work during the Sino-Soviet Alliance period was the Chinese Academy of Sciences, established in 1949. Today, it takes on a much more elaborate multi-group form with a less desirable name: the Chinese Academy of Sciences Holdings (CASH). It remains one of the leading national-level science and research organizations that are

responsible for making industrial towns in various parts of China. In particular, the Jiading New Town in Shanghai, planned and built in the early 1960s, was part of this study. In the contemporary period, as a northernmost district of Shanghai, Jiading New Town continues to grow into a city of one million residents. This study includes an experimental adaptive reuse of one of Jiading's laboratories from the Sino-Soviet Alliance period, built as part of China's technological revolution at the onset of the Cold War. Jiading was designated a Science Town, incorporating universities and many laboratories and buildings focused on research and development.

The second study is the Shanghai Automotive Industry Corporation (SAIC Motor). Since its modest beginnings in 1955 as the Shanghai Internal Combustion Engine Components Company, it would evolve through the policies and disruptions of the Cultural Revolution and the Great Leap Forward, and emerge as a critical player in the automobile industry in China. The automobile was seen as a symbol of progress in Communist China, which explains why it was selected as a key industry to propel China forward. It led to the growth of peripheral industrial areas near the urban core of Shanghai. The Pengpu and Taopu industrial districts were key urban sites for the production and assembly of automobile parts. Such districts also benefitted from the development of infrastructure such as railways and new road networks to assist the industry's production lines and their connection to river ports. Worker housing in the form of communes was also dispersed among the urban factories, taking advantage of the original village settlements that existed in the area. This building stock has evolved into creative offices as the car industry was reconsolidated, with German and other global partners, in the district of Anting. Districts such as Pengpu would gradually change into spaces of consumption, offices, and commercial functions. The piecemeal reconstruction of the district would inherit the odd pockets of space, which carried the traces of industrial activities as well as a wealth of localized domestic, commercial, and work functions.

The third study is the Caohejing Hi-Tech Industrial Park, which was developed in 1982 as a flagship district of the Economic and Technological Development Zone (ETDZ) policy. It was positioned as one of eleven elite, national-level, high-tech industrial parks, with special policies not only to incentivize the entry of global multinational corporations, but also to promote rapid urbanization.

Added together, these organizations and sites offer insights into many inherent contradictions in the explosion of industrialization, modernization, urbanization, and globalization. The specific site and policy conditions are carefully documented to reveal a series of new urban functions, problematic environmental issues, and uncanny juxtapositions of social, economic, and global classes. These conditions would lead to innovative designs represented at an architectural scale as well. Four architectural projects are also represented to demonstrate how these ideas come together to impact everyday life. This study demonstrates that the industrial type is no longer the typological form familiar in European and United States historical cases. In China, the emergent socio-political, technological, and environmental conditions would give rise to unique organizations and forms.

Shenzhen
Shenzhen to PRD Method
Jason Hilgefort
Merve Bedir (Future + Aformal Academy)

The notion of Shenzhen "speed" has led to a way of thinking about, learning about, and operating the productive city in the last thirty years. Today, this method includes a dispersed network of rapid manufacturing and logistics throughout the Pearl River Delta (PRD).

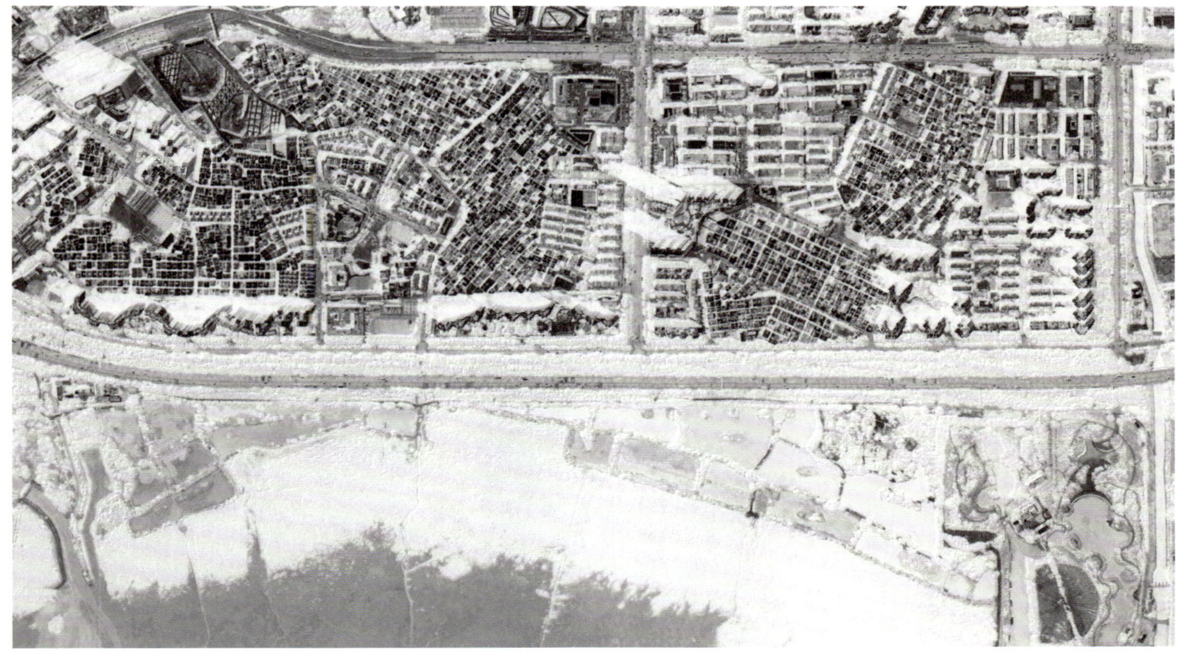

Shawei aerial view, 2017 © Jason Hilgefort

Huaqiangbei Electronics Market, 2016 © Merve Bedirfort

In the PRD, design emerges from networked incrementalism, where diverse producers work in competition and collaboration, creating a collective and dynamic process of composing based on a highly efficient digital and physical infrastructure of communication and distribution. In addition, the culture of craftsmanship, as well as the global shift to a (free) market economy and the economies of scale, holds the context to the PRD method.

In the Shawei urban village, we mapped the local resources, and provided space for—and facilitated collaboration between—international and local designers to work within the community. The Shawei section of the exhibition presents the value of the MICRO system of production in Shenzhen; the PRD section of the exhibition presents the dispersed MACRO system of production in the Greater Pearl River Delta Region. We visualized production facilities in general, displaying the economies of scale in the PRD. Lastly, the Huaqiangbei Electronics Market is documented and presented as an emblematic marketplace of this system, its methodology of production, and mode of learning.

Linking "design" (Shenzhen government's desired outcome) and the city's existing conditions (perceived as disposable) provides greater value for both; it reframes the lens for the government, citizens, and design community to re-evaluate their city. The PRD Method asks for the necessary connections between production and design in urban space, in pursuit of the future city.

Singapore
White Space

Keng Hua Chong
Singapore University of Technology and
Design (SUTD)

After a year-long Jubilee celebration of Singapore's independence in 2015, current urban planning and design often imply an attitude or vision of what the city-state could become in the next fifty years. The success of its planning in the past was never an accident, but represented conscious efforts toward creating new spaces through land reclamation, urban regeneration, densification, and vertical expansion (both upwards and downwards).

Despite optimizing every square meter of livable space, a large number of urban voids exist in the city, awaiting future development. These voids—intentionally carved out "white spaces" within the urban fabric or building complexes—have the potential for spatial or programmatic experiments to take place.

The Singapore Pavilion thus takes this concept of "white space" further and seeks to test out new spatial typologies in response to emerging socio-economic issues in Singapore, going beyond the usual zoning guidelines of residential, industrial, or commercial. We identify four main challenges or opportunities: Demographic transformation, Information revolution, Resource redistribution, Production reform. These are by no means stand-alone initiatives; all are interlinked, forming a complex urban condition.

Void deck under a housing block appropriated as a birds' club for seniors.
© Photo by Chong Keng Hua

Leftover space under train tracks. © Photo by Chong Keng Hua

The design of the pavilion is generated through the subtraction of a rectangular volume, giving rise to a series of void spaces that await interventions while allowing visitors to flow through. Lattices made of the ubiquitous bamboo poles found in every public housing block represent the basic building blocks of city and high-rise structures. The folded aluminum composite panels that hug the lattice surfaces showcase eight strategies, each one dealing with one or more of the pressing issues mentioned above.

Through the confluence of environment, people, and technology, diverse yet targeted experiments are applied to put their limits to the test. With these white spaces, we envision Singapore becoming a prototype for the world.

TERROIR
Office of the NSW Government Architect

The Seoul Biennale curators suggest that a new cosmology and new cosmopolitics are required in this age of the Anthropocene—a claim that demands a response and perhaps also a strategy for engagement from the discipline of architecture. If we accept Pier Vittorio Aureli's duality—that a political project is also spatial, while a spatial project is also political—it follows that the new cosmology and cosmopolitics cannot be brought into existence without significant rethinking of the relationship between resources (commons) and their situation in space.

There is no question of the discipline's capacity to make a profound contribution to this remaking of the world; rather, the dilem-

© Courtesy of Transport for NSW.

ma is whether there is an inclination to participate. The issues the curators raise are not in themselves new, but they can be understood as increasing in urgency. Despite this, the architectural profession continues to focus its disciplinary self-image on the production of objects, while a political project of this scale must be met with a spatial engagement that operates at a scale larger than any particular building.

The philosopher Andrew Benjamin, in *Towards a Relational Ontology*, provides a conceptual framework that can assist architecture in addressing its potential in this regard. Benjamin tracks the concept of a relational ontology as a fundamental premise through the history of philosophy: "Relationality describes a state of affairs that is ontological. It is not just that being is relational, but that what exists fundamentally is a relation."[10] The singular, in this sense, cannot exist by itself, for "singulars are always already in relation such that singularities are the after-effect of relationality."[11]

The "object to network" repositioning suggested by Benjamin immediately talks to the unrealized power of the discipline as a spatial practice, which fundamentally deals in the projection of possible outcomes through reorganizing relations in space. The relations we talk of may be broad in scope and can be understood and implemented at multiple scales, enabling future projections of the world where a redistribution of commons may be possible. David Cunningham is in accord with this proposed reorientation, noting: "On a planet housing seven billion people, forms of mediation, abstraction, and impersonality are not only ineliminable, but are necessary to the construction of new social relations and modes of collective transformation of our increasingly urbanised world."

But this transformation is not just a matter of reorienting the discipline's self-image. The question of the client-driven nature of professional practice also arises, as does how society may be served by a different professional formation of architectural practice, focused on

something other than the hero-author. Another inevitable question: How might architecture engage with the state, and what is the role of the state in this new cosmopolitics? As David Harvey bluntly puts it, while revolution is quite properly opposed to prevailing notions of the republic of property, the presumption that the world's seven billion people can be fed, warmed, clothed, housed and cleaned without any hierarchical form of governance, and outside the reach of monetization or markets, is dubious in the extreme. The question is far too huge to be left to the horizontal self-organization of autonomous beings.

Concerns regarding the capacity of government to truly redirect resources in the age of neoliberal managerialism, and the current impossibility of reaching large-scale consensus on key issues such as climate change, leave city-scale governance as perhaps the most viable arena for consequential action. A "city architect" thus becomes, subject to the configuration of that role and its independence to give advice, an actor who may sit at

© TERROIR

10. Andrew Benjamin, *Towards a Relational Ontology* (Albany: State University of New York Press) 2015. Kindle ebook loc 407.
11. Ibid. loc 420.

the confluence of the disciplinary and political leverage necessary to effect change.

This installation provides a window into the development of one such scenario: a collaboration between the Government Architect's office of New South Wales and private architectural practice. Together with the profession, the Government Architect is developing a design-led methodology for place-based spatial strategies that organize people, resources, and space at the scale of the precinct. A key opportunity of the work is the embedding of these strategies and resultant logics into political processes and planning systems through a document known as a Spatial Framework.

Spatial Frameworks attempts a synthesis of spatial intelligence with substantial engagement processes across the political and bureaucratic realms in order to foster the equitable distribution of commons. This model holds the possibility of the reorganization of relations—and thus the enactment of a new cosmology and cosmopolitics—through an alignment between a political project and a specific spatial context. The political agency of the Spatial Framework document thus exists not only in what is proposed, but in the after-effects of the process itself. A change in the subjectivity of those who govern is of course the first move necessary if we are to seriously address the age of the anthropocene.

Tehran
Cultivating Tehran
Amin Tadjsoleiman
Tehran Urban Innovation Center (TUIC)

Not very long ago, Tehran was a small village surrounded by gardens, watered by the seven ravines passing through the city from the northern mountains. Fast modernization has changed the city's relationship to its rural land and food production chains. The growing city has erased most of its lands and gardens; however, this valuable agriculture infrastructure is still there. Tehran has some of the highest average precipitation among the major cities of Iran, and it has a network of streams and aqueducts running under and through the city. Simultaneously with a cultural shift regarding urban farming, an emerging social group of newcomer farmers is developing in the city. By including the skills of this

Implementing farming/housing unit in Tehran's leftover spaces © Amin Tadjsoleiman

growing social group into the city structure, the food production chain in Tehran can be more efficient and resilient.

Potential: Leftover Urban Spaces as Possible Sites for Bottom-up Food Production and Distribution

As rising buildings and urban infrastructure are replacing farmlands, new potential cultivatable surfaces are appearing. The available urban surfaces are the setbacks of ravines and urban infrastructure, unplanned and vacant lands, common spaces and roofs of large blocks, as well as underused or less-frequented public parks. A few of these spaces are already being used informally for agriculture, and their products are distributed through a network of food carts.

Proposal: A Hybrid, Integrated, Networked, Bottom-Up, and Human-Centered Platform for Urban Farming Revival

As proposed to the City of Tehran, through deployment of a three-layered urban farming system, the city can become more resilient in regards to food resources. The first layer includes a network of cultivatable patches of leftover space in the city. The second layer is based on a trackable network of pop-up farming units that serve as production and distribution hubs. The third layer is an application based on social media platforms for making urban farms operate in an interconnected network and in relation to their customers.

Tijuana / San Diego
Living Borders

Rene Peralta

The region nested between the city of San Diego (SD) in the United States and Tijuana (TJ) in Mexico is one of the most dynamic border spaces in the Americas. A paradoxical effect between the two cities allows them to maintain their uniqueness, and at the same time produces a region that strives for prosperous cultural and economic interaction.

Today, the border is a contested landscape in political, economic and ecological terms. The current political rhetoric of the Trump administration regarding the promise to build a longer and taller border wall seems to be defied by the present flow of economic and cultural exchanges between San Diego and Tijuana. Economic trade between the cities is estimated at $4 billion a year in a region of five million people and two million workers. At the onset of the twenty-first century, the border region between the cities is home to one of the most traveled land ports in the world, with approximately 60,000 pedestrians and 130,000 vehicles crossing every day.

The intrinsic differences between the two sides of this 169-year-old border have had a significant effect on the production of a hybridized culture and way of life. Yet, both cities are part of a shared geography that includes a diverse set of ecosystems that do not follow the logic of nation-states or political borders.

© Rene Peralta

The region nested between the city of San Diego and Tijuana.

S.O.S.
Se están yendo las
empresas de Tijuana
Genaro
Lopez

For example, water is a shared element that crosses the border at several places and is part of the precious natural resources that require binational and cross-border attention.

The unique identity of each city is based on differing visions of city planning. Tijuana is a city of expediency, where the urban is built every day, while San Diego is a slower city, where decisions are part of a regulatory and administrative system. Part of this differentiation in planning is that Tijuana is essentially a Latin American city, with a strong economic center near the border and concentric sectors radiating out to its worker and industrial neighborhoods. As for San Diego, it tends to be organized as a series of subcenters that sprawl along the California coast line.

The future of this region relies on the continuation of the active socio-economic exchanges between the two cities; however, the most important thing is the need to promote the joint care of the fragile ecosystem that sustains the livability of this semi-arid region.

The SD/TJ border region is not defined as, or intending to reach, a state of integration; its mode of operation seems to be one of interaction where both sides are continually shaping a unique identity based on their confluence.

Tokyo
Common Matters
Keigo Kobayashi + K2LAB
Christian Dimmer (Waseda University)

The old, growth-obsessed Japan of the 1980s and 1990s was synonymous with an insatiable hunger for passive, individualized consumerism and commodification of the life-world. Today, neighborhoods like Tokyo's historic Yanaka have transformed into flourishing social laboratories, with community innovators, civic-minded entrepreneurs, local decision makers, socially engaged artists, and local residents experimenting with alternative practices and lifestyles.

Often the producers of these community projects are unaware of, or not explicit about, the larger (political) implications of providing new social and economic models for Japan's nascent post-growth society. But where peo-

Ueno Sakuragi Atari, a preserved neighborhood corner turned into a local's common space. © Keigo Kobayashi Lab

ple explore new forms of social relations, collaboration, decision making, cultural practices, or human experience beyond state and market logic, they prefigure a more democratic, pluralistic, and sustainable society.

Community innovators are often motivated individuals with high levels of social capital; they seek to enrich their personal lives beyond the constraints of corporate Japan and to find individual happiness and meaning. What often starts as a personal impulse and a strong commitment to a locality leads to individual empowerment and creates intersections with other similarly socially engaged producers. At these meeting points new common worlds emerge.

The Yanaka neighborhood cuts across the borders of three different Tokyo boroughs. Somehow the margins of three local governments created a vacuum that allowed civic activism to flourish. Yanaka is a new place identity that was assembled through one of Japan's first place-based citizen magazines, launched in 1984 by community activists. In a time of skyrocketing land prices and a seemingly unstoppable redevelopment frenzy, the activists sought to create a common purpose by rediscovering local histories and cultures and mobilizing against outside pressure.

The materiality of the place and its specific history are vital for understanding the open and innovative atmosphere in the neighborhood and the existence of many common matters.

Few other places in central Tokyo escaped direct destruction during the Great Kanto

122

Earthquake of 1923 and the Allied carpet bombing of 1945. The extensive greenery of temples and cemeteries—concentrated here after a large fire devastated the overcrowded city center in the seventeenth century—had protected the area and preserved its fine-grained spatial structure. The dense web of narrow back alleys and micro-scale open spaces prevented extensive redevelopment activities and led to the existence of a large stock of older buildings, which would later become a common matter for preservationists.

In this old temple town the residents were long accustomed to welcoming a constant flow of pilgrims. Due to this influx of visitors, unique crafts and services emerged, and a hospitable and open atmosphere evolved.

While historical processes and its spatial setting make Yanaka unique and help to bring about a very distinct local culture, it has many things in common with other parts of Tokyo. Everywhere in urban Japan communities are similarly experimenting, for example, with new economic models that are needed to deal with the country's shrinking and rapidly greying population. Everywhere, local innovators search for solutions to filling the empty buildings and vacant spaces that have opened up in an age of depopulation and post-growth. Everywhere in Japan and beyond, communities are searching for more sustainable and fulfilling forms of life.

The term "commons" is often used to characterize a more or less coherent community of people who share a specific resource and safeguard its fair use.

The twenty-one elements presented here are representative of the wide and rich spectrum of community projects and big and small commons in Yanaka. They are ordinary, everyday matters that show diverse motivations and strong individual aspirations, as well as the desire to collaborate with others; these are vital prerequisites to creating and maintaining the commons.

Community and commons don't exist a priori, nor are "commoners" born as such. They co-emerge with common matters that

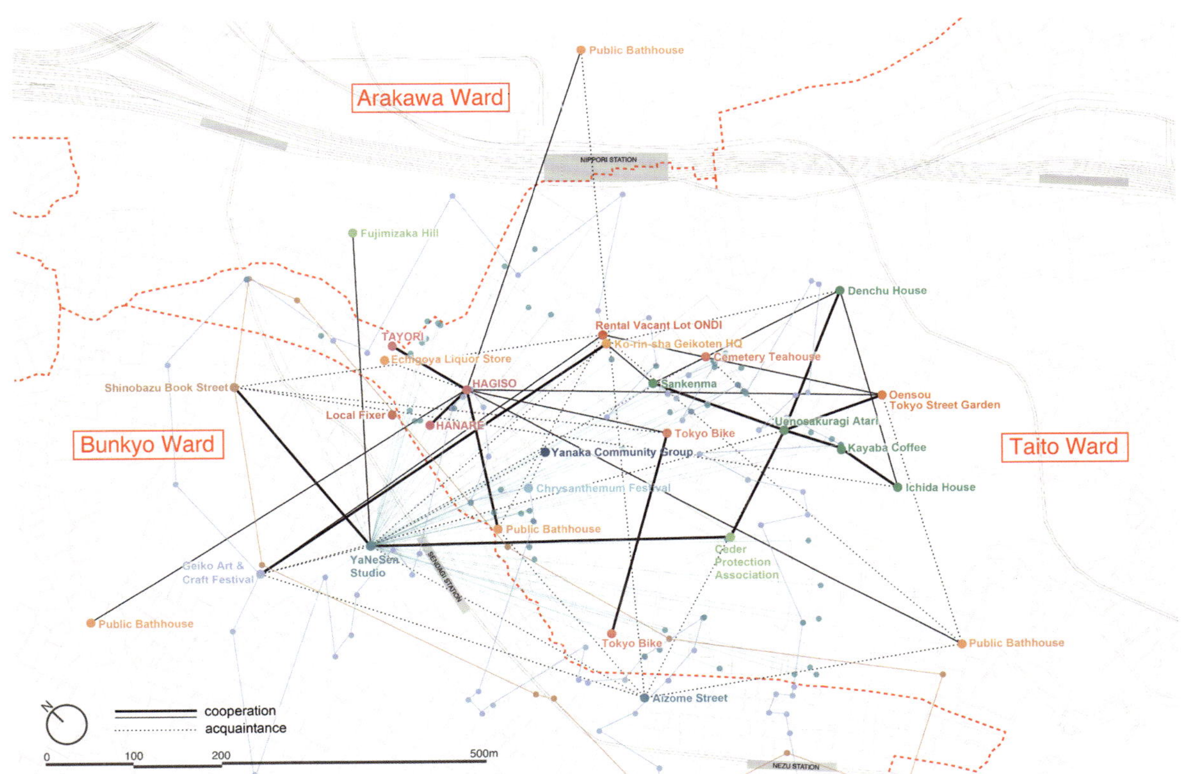

Map of Yanaka area with locations of activities and relationships. © Keigo Kobayashi Lab

connect people and places. Rather than monolithic and unitary, commons coexist and co-emerge at various levels; nestled into one another, larger commons are assembled by smaller ones, each of them dynamically expanding, contracting, or fusing with others.

This nuanced view of the commons suggests that it is not necessary to coerce everyone into a unified, common mindset, but rather it is necessary to allow and embrace the coexistence of a variety of motives, loosely connected to each other by big and small common matters. In pluralistic societies a collection of independent actions with self-empowered, strong, intrinsic motivations is important to create sustainable projects and to foster creativity.

Vienna
The Vienna Model
Wolfgang Förster
IBA Vienna

Social Housing Policies in Vienna, Austria: A Contribution to Social Cohesion

For a long time the Austrian capital Vienna has been well known for its tradition of social housing. This article explains how social housing policies in Vienna have developed into an integrated system of technical and social urban planning.

Decentralized Housing Policies

Written into the federal constitution of Austria, the nine Bundesländer (provinces) enjoy a certain freedom in formulating their housing policies. Vienna, which is also a province, differs considerably from the rest of the country, as it is Austria's only metropolitan area.

Secure Financing

The financing of social housing, both in the rental sector and in the subsidized owner-occupied and single-family housing sectors, is based on contributions from national taxes and from the regional budget. The national tax revenues are distributed to the nine provinces according to a complex financial agreement; Vienna receives approximately 450 million each year for housing subsidies.

Despite several cuts in recent years, this way of financing still provides a secure base for the planning of social housing programs on a large scale, which would not be possible under strictly market-oriented housing policies. The city itself, however, has had to contribute further means from its own budgets in recent years due to an increased demand for housing. Thus, the total expenditure for housing subsidies is some 600 million each year. Although this subsidization of housing with tax income is to some extent dependent on overall economic conditions, subsidies such as these directly influence the production of new housing—contrary to tax-deduction models used in many countries, which primarily benefit better-off households. Besides, the total expenditure for housing expressed as a percentage of the GDP is significantly lower than in countries that focus on indirect subsidies by tax deduction.

Due to the expected growth of the population from 1.7 million to some 1.9 to 2 million within the next fifteen years, the subsidized housing program has now been increased from 5,000 to 7,000 units per year.

Limited-Profit Housing

As Austria's biggest landlord, the city of Vienna owns about 220,000 rental apartments. Still, in recent years, the major portion of new social housing has been carried out by limited-profit housing associations under varying legal conditions. These associations are subject to the national Limited-Profit Housing Act, and to a second control by their own corporations as well as their respective provincial governments. At present, about two hundred limited-profit housing associations are active in Austria, managing some 650,000 apartments and building another 15,000 every year. In Vienna, they own and manage about 136,000 apartments, in addition to the city's own 220,000; most of the owner-occupied apartments have been built within the subsidized housing program. These owner-occupied apartments are therefore also subject to certain limitations concerning the income per household and the later sale of the apartments. Limited-profit housing associations enjoy tax abatements and have to re-invest profits back into housing. Rents are strictly regulated: the cost-rent covers financing, the running costs, and the 10% value-added tax (consumer tax). The maximum monthly net-rent for a subsidized apartment in Vienna is currently about 4.50 euros per square meter, or 6 to 7 per square meter in total. Low-income households are entitled to housing allowances, ensuring that they do not lose their apartments in case of a sudden illness or unemployment.

To reduce financing costs, most developers ask for a down payment, which for rental housing may not exceed 12.5% of the total construction costs, as well as a share in the cost of the land. These tenant contributions are refunded with interest when the tenants move out. Low-income households are entitled to low-interest public loans or even to apartments without a down payment. All subsidized apartments are subject to certain income limits at the time of completion; high-income households are mostly excluded from such housing, for example. However, a later increase of income does not lead to a loss of the apartment.

Direct and Individual Subsidies

The federal constitution allows Vienna to set its own criteria for housing subsidies more or less autonomously; object subsidies are given to the developers in order for them to reduce the financing costs and rents. Typically, the amount of non-repayable subsidies is around 30% of the total construction costs. Meanwhile, with regard to European Union regulations, such grants have been replaced by public 1% interest loans of up to thirty-five years. The level of grants depends on the project, with higher subsidies given to special projects like passive housing (housing estates without any sort of traditional heating) and other environmentally conscious developments. As opposed to individual grants, these subsidies give the public administration the possibility to directly influence housing production. Still, the percentage of subsidies to the tenants is increasing, and now low-income households even have a legal right to receive such allowances.

Reducing Construction Costs

All subsidized housing projects are subject to a public bidding process, with the best offer (not necessarily the cheapest) to be commissioned. Presently, total construction costs, including those for planning, amount to approximately 1,600 euros per square meter of useable floor space, plus an amount for the respective share of land costs. Higher land prices are usually not accepted for social housing purposes. The city of Vienna profits from its strong influence on the land market due to the high percentage—approximately 90%—of social housing within the total housing production, and due to the dedicated use of large areas exclusively for housing purposes. Developer competitions, organized for all the larger projects, also help to reduce construction costs. Developers have to offer a complete product, consisting of the planning, ecological measures, social sustainability, and exact economic calculations, and they are judged along this "four-pillar system" by an interdisciplinary jury using a complex scoring system. Developers have to give a price guarantee, otherwise they risk losing the subsidies!

Ecology

As a result of several experimental buildings, low-energy consumption (about 35 kilowatts per square meter per year) has now become the rule in new housing, with more and more housing reaching the passive house standard (less than 15 kilowatts per square meter per year). This is also seen as one of Vienna's contributions to fulfilling the requirements of the Kyoto Treaty. Other ecological measures include individual water metering, the use of rainwater and "grey" water, passive and active solar energy use, and measures to reduce emissions from construction sites.

New housing estates are required to connect to the city-owned district heating system; as far as technically feasible, this is also the case with all subsidized renewal projects. Currently, some 212,000 apartments—about 25% of all housing in Vienna—as well as a large number of offices and business premises are connected to this heating system. It comprises 900 kilometers of pipe. Each apartment is

Wohnpark Alt-Erlaa. © Hertha Hurnaus

Karl-Marx-Hof. © Stadt Wien / City of Vienna, 2013

metered individually. The initial temperature lies between 95 and 150 degrees Celsius depending on the outside temperature. About 25% of the necessary energy is provided by waste incineration; the rest comes from linkages to several power stations and a large refinery. Only at peak times does the deficit have to be produced. The five gas or oil power stations that are drawn on generate only about 4.5% of annual consumption. Thus, 64.6% of all primary energy can be saved, equaling a reduction of carbon dioxide (CO_2) output of one million tons. The present capacity of the district heating company is being extended continuously.

Tenants' Security

Despite much controversy, the 1917 Tenancy Act, which regulates the maximum amount of rent that may be asked for an apartment according to location, legal status, and construction period, has remained a national law up to the present day. Only in very few, precisely defined cases, can rents be increased. Limited rental contracts have been allowed for some years. Most Vienna households nevertheless benefit from indefinite rental contracts, which can even be passed on to children occupying the same flat. In social housing, only indefinite contracts are permitted, and tenants enjoy broad participation in the day-to-day management of the building. In privately owned rental buildings, too, tenants are guaranteed important rights; they may, for example, carry out improvements against the owner's wishes (but not the other way round!). Disagreements between landlords and tenants can be decided by a city-run arbitration office at no extra cost. The decisions of this department are legally binding and can be passed on to the courts. This unusually high security for tenants may explain why about 80% of all Vienna residents live in rental apartments.

Balanced Neighborhoods

In order to prevent the emergence of social ghettos, new housing areas usually comprise apartments of different costs and of various legal statuses: rental and owner-occupied apartments with higher or lower subsidies, as well as privately financed condominiums without any income limits. As a result, large new housing estates have a rather good social mixture.

Allocation

Within the subsidized housing program, two forms of housing have to be distinguished: council housing (which is less expensive), and housing provided by nonprofit associations or other developers using public subsidies. In the latter, income limits are higher, making these estates accessible for a large part of the population. Developers also offer some flats for home-ownership, with a slightly higher income limit. Applications for council housing follow a strict score system (urgency of demand, size of household, etc.) which is transparent for all applicants. All developers using public subsidies have to give one-third of the new apartments to the city for allocation, which then follows the same principles as in council housing; the rest of the subsidized flats are let or sold by the associations themselves.

Social City Planning

In Vienna, housing is understood as a part of social-oriented city planning. The city has installed an infrastructure commission to define in detail the conditions for subsidized housing projects. Thus, new housing projects form a part of an existing system and help to overcome infrastructure deficiencies, such as schools or health institutions, for example. Public means of transport are equally important.

The general rules are put down in the City Development Plan, which is revised and adopted by the City Council roughly every ten years. It defines the general aims and the development trends, including the housing or business zones, axes of urban development along public transport lines, and green areas, among other concerns. Other plans, notably the Land Use Plan, are based on this general model.

The Land Use Plan is subject to broad public participation by residents and district councils; it is also adopted by the City Council. It includes the exactly defined use of each single plot in Vienna. These plans are worked out by the respective City Planning Departments (MA 21A and B) and by the politicians (councillors) who bear the responsibility for urban planning and housing.

Social Architecture

The general policy of Vienna to not leave urban development and housing completely up to the free market is complemented by the housing subsidies and by the regulations of the Building Order, a Vienna provincial act. In its first part, this law regulates issues of city planning, like the interdisciplinary Advisory Board for Urban Planning and Urban Development, and the contents of the Land Use Plan. These plans have to describe in detail the exact use for each plot of land, the height and form of the buildings (free-standing, attached, etc.), the maximum density, the number of green areas and underground building sections among others. They are legally binding for everyone after adoption by the City Council.

Other chapters of the Building Order law stipulate technical requirements, such as health protection and handicapped accessibility, as well as the architectural design. Without impeding modern architecture, even in so-called protection zones, any disturbance of the overall urban landscape should be prevented. The city has its own architectural department (MA 19) to provide advice and to offer assistance in deciding about new buildings, reconstruction, or the design of open areas. The department has also collected data about culturally valuable buildings, which can be accessed via the internet.

Information and Public Discourse

A further development of social housing concerns urban planning, architecture, ecology, and—last but not least—social policy. This needs an ongoing broad discussion among the general public and experts, as well as continuous information availability. This includes special housing research programs and the distribution of their results by publications, presentations, and regular reporting on hous-

© JO Jaemoo

ing issues in the media. Of course, the clients of social housing, potential house-hunters, for example, have to be informed comprehensively and without bureaucratic obstacles. At the city-owned company Wohnservice Wien, all information about planned and completed subsidized housing projects can be obtained at its centrally located service center or via its web page. But this is only the beginning. The city is now implementing its e-government strategy, which in the near future will enable residents to carry out all necessary steps from their homes, from the first overview of new housing, to the reservation of a particular apartment.

Vienna's social housing thus represents a manifold system, which for decades has continuously developed and adapted to meet new challenges. In spite of its complexity, however, its primary aim is always kept in mind: to offer comfortable contemporary housing in an attractive urban environment to all residents at affordable prices.

Yeongju
Multiple Systems of Urban-Rural Integrated City: Yeongju's Public Architecture Masterplan
Yeongju City

Yeongju is an inland city in the far north region of North Gyeongsang province in South Korea. As a typical *do-nong* (urban-rural) city, it was one of the cities that vividly illustrated the classic case of a declining small-to-mid-size municipality outside of the Seoul area after the 1990s. However, in 2010, for the first time at the level of a local government, Yeongju City established a design management team charged with the task of establishing and implementing relevant policies. The team's work became vital as the city was truly revived. The city is working hard to manage and implement an integrated approach to public design. These efforts are organized around four themes: urban regeneration, history, housing quality, and culture and sports. The exhibition will convey the approach of the four themes and the impact of the initiative on the different districts of the city.

In the first section "Urban Regeneration," the exhibition focuses on the transformation of the village Samgakji ("delta village"). It is an urban neighborhood that became an island unto itself. It had fallen behind the times after it was physically cut off from the rest of the city by the three railroad tracks passing through the city. The transformation of the village is highlighted by two new projects: a welfare center for senior citizens and a welfare center for the disabled. Samgakji Green Street is the newly designated name for the transformed area. The exhibition also introduces the way Husaeng *sijang* and Haksa *golmok* are being reorganized: the former is a traditional market and the latter is an alleyway near a local college campus popular among young people.

The second theme, the "History" section, introduces the overall urban changes of the main street in the old downtown area. Due to structural changes in local industries and the aging population, the downtown area has been declining rapidly. The city is seeking to utilize public spaces in the area in various ways. There are now streets with special themes of "history and culture." Visitors to the area will find, for example, a neighborhood community center in a *hanok* (traditional Korean-style building) that also serves as a local "food experience hall." There is also a B-boy performance space for the young. Thirdly, the "Housing Quality" section reviews improvements in residential environments and neighborhood revitalization programs. Jo-se Health Care Center, Pungi-eup Office, and Gwansagol Elderly Center are the various pilot design projects under the program. Lastly, in the "Culture and Sports" section, the exhibition introduces the city plan for an indoor swimming pool, a Boxing Association of Korea gym, and a central library for the city. These facilities will connect public spaces with public service programs in front of city hall. There is also a video made by Efraín Méndez, a Spanish architectural filmmaker and photographer, containing scenes from around Yeongju and its public architecture. Archival materials on public architecture from other cities are also presented.

Homo Urbanus
Bêka & Lemoine

This work is a long-term research project developed until now in five different cities over the world: Seoul, Bogota, Naples, Saint-Petersburg and Rabat. The project is an evolving filmic work, which will have different forms at each steps of its development. The video installation conceived for the Seoul Biennale is the first public showing of this work in a condensed version.

Born as an artistic commission for the Agora Biennale in Bordeaux 2017 on the theme of the moving landscapes, this work proposes a very subjective immersion into cities aiming to translate in the closest possible way the feel of their constant moving nature — their human landscape.

Presented in a comparative dynamic through the lens of a selection of themes and issues linked with the street daily life, the videos enable us to perceive each of these different urban contexts as an experimental, local and unique laboratory answering the same global challenge of how can we live all together.

Walking in unknown cities to collect impressions, to catch a vibration, to gather situations and scenes observed at the angle of a street, on a crossroad or from the top of a building. Depicting a city in its present, in the simplicity of its daily life. Listening to its rumble, the sound of its depths. Slipping into its rhythm. To be on the lookout, in a continuous wonder towards the imagination and creativity men have managed to develop to find a way to live together.

Asking ourselves: What makes a city? Trying to understand its silent rules, its habits, its imperfections, its difficulties, and its unique way to answer the endless question: Where do we go? These visual notes, made on the fly, look at the urban inhabitant within his group and in his deep solitude, redrawing the outline of each city following a sentimental geography.

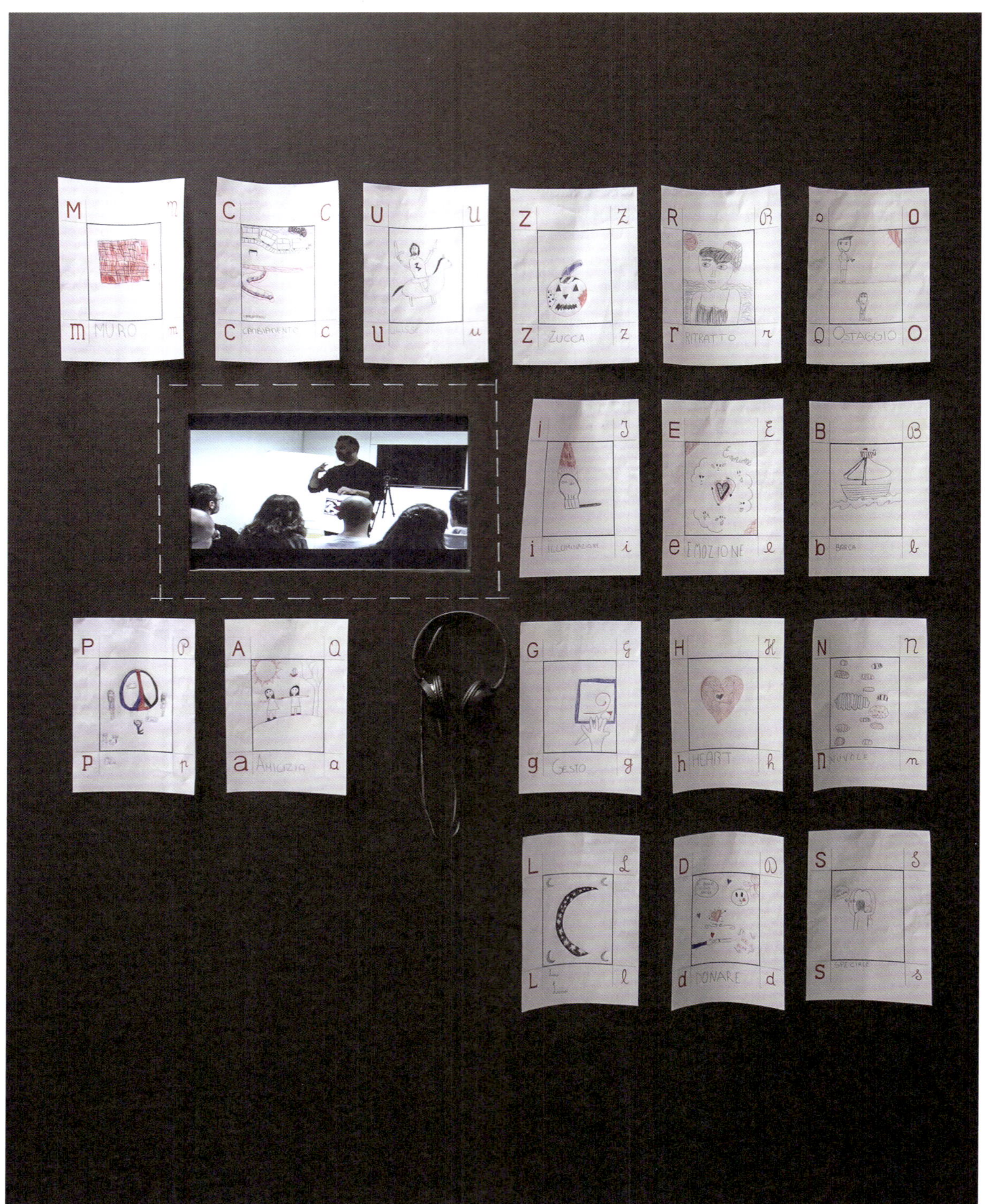

© Giuseppe Stampone

Toward a (Dis)-Educating City: The (Dis)-Educational Workshop
Giuseppe Stampone

Productivity-centric and consumer-centric cultures emulating, or belonging to, Europe and the United States suffer from paradoxical and optimistic short-sightedness, which causes their relationship with the environment to be reduced to a mere functional exchange. Their interaction with nature becomes an indiscriminate pillage of resources; it is to treat nature itself as a decorative backdrop, a holiday setting, a domesticated exoticism adorning private spaces and certain areas within urban spaces.

While all this occurs, unbeknownst to the majority and yet with everyone responsible for it, the crisis originating from this exploitation is at the root of most humanitarian crises, social conflicts, and catastrophes now affecting the planet on a global scale.

An artist's work, aware of the fact that changes on a larger scale stem from individual choices and actions, is more and more clearly oriented toward practices, transformative gestures, and new situations that infuse the individual with a sense of responsibility and a new respect for his/her position vis-à-vis local and global management policies. Giuseppe Stampone's *Architectures of Intelligence* are set precisely in this perspective, involving less conventional authors and actors in a creative process at the heart of which lies a strong educational purpose.

These are complex operations that put together educational strategies strongly based on a peer-to-peer relationship between interlocutors, where the didactic process, reciprocal listening, and collective and individual effort constitute the essence of artistic creation. The visible, "formal sediment" that becomes consolidated in the final display is only a result of intelligent energy generated in the process—intelligence as substance, engine, and backdrop for these processes, held up by the relationships between subjects and the connections they are capable of triggering.

Inspired by Rem Koolhaas's sentence that describes the South Korean capital as "Manhattan with Alps," Stampone creates a new "Architecture of Intelligence" based on the relationship between urban spaces and their surrounding ecosystems. Seoul, one of the major and most sophisticated cities in Asia, where the most advanced technologies and the environment try to walk hand in hand, is what gave Stampone the idea for a group map as part of his recent research. He asked ten people—artists and intellectuals who are close to him in terms of ethical vocation and project sharing—to come up with ten proposals that will be put on a larger conceptual map. The focus of the action is the "areas of weakness" between the city and natural environment, spaces that resemble Marc Augé's "non-places" and Gilles Clement's concept of the Third Landscape. Here the attrition between civilization and environment is more present, the balance more delicate and unstable, and the consequences of each choice more serious. Together with the map, Stampone created a children's workshop to put together a spelling book in Korean, which is displayed next to a video illustrating the entire process and the group map, to which the following people contributed: Stefano Boccalino, Jota Castro, Pietro Gaglianò, Igor Grubic, Ugo La Pietra, Margherita Moscardini, Marco Neri, OBRA Architects, Paolo Parisi, Simona Pavone, Alfredo Pirri, RAVE (Isabella Pers and Tiziana Pers), Lorenzo Scotto di Luzio, Bernardì Roig, Marinella Senatore, Eugenio Tibaldi.

Editors

Helen Hejung Choi is an Assistant Professor at Kookmin Unversity, Seoul, Korea. After completing her Masters degree in Architectural Design at Columbia University, she has participated in numerous public housing projects and initiatives with Non-Profit Organizations in New York City. Since 2005, she has moved to Seoul teaching and practicing as architecture professor, researcher, and curator. She was a curator for the Gwangju Design Biennale in 2011, and the head researcher for Architecture in Asia collection for the Archive and Research Library Park at the Asian Culture Complex in Gwangju in 2014.

Hyungmin Pai is a historian, critic, and curator. A two-time Fulbright Scholar, he received his Ph.D at MIT and teaches at the University of Seoul. He is author of *The Portfolio and the Diagram, Sensuous Plan: The Architecture of Seung H-Sang, and The Key Concepts of Korean Architecture*. For the Venice Biennale, he was twice curator for the Korean Pavilion (awarded the Golden Lion, 2014) and a participant in the Common Pavilions (2012). He was Chief Curator for the Gwangju Design Biennale and guest curator for numerous international exhibitions. He is the Director of the inaugural Seoul Biennale of Architecture and Urbanism.

Authors / Artists / Organizations

History of City Planning — From the "Functional City" to "Total Function": Planning the Modern City, 1925–1971

Annie Pedret is an Associate Professor at Seoul National University. She has taught the history and theory of architecture and studios at the Illinois Institute of Technology and the University of Illinois at Chicago. Her research focuses on post–World War II modern architecture, post-Socialist Pyongyang and the role of the historian in envisioning urban futures. She is the author of *Team 10: An Archival History* (2013). She has lectured internationally about CIAM and Team 10 and the method of scenario planning in architecture. She completed her BSc at the University of Toronto, BArch at the University of British Columbia, and S.M.Arch.S. and PhD degrees in architectural history and theory at MIT.

Cities in Comparison — Dynamics of the Urban Age

LSE Cities is an international center supported by Deutsche Bank at the London School of Economics and Political Science. LSE Cities carries out research, conferences, graduate and executive education, and outreach activities internationally. Its mission is to study how people and cities interact in a rapidly urbanizing world, focusing on how the physical form and design of cities impacts on society, culture, and the environment.

Amsterdam — Amsterdam Approach

An urban designer by profession, Eric van der Kooij is also a strategic adviser and the head of spatial quality for the Department of Spatial Planning and Sustainability of the City of Amsterdam, where he has worked for almost twenty years. His team is responsible for stimulating spatial quality and knowledge exchange.

The department focuses on developing, designing, and controlling spatial developments on all relevant scales of the metropolitan area and the city in an integrated approach, by means of strategies, master planning, adaptive approaches, policies, and guidelines. The department is in constant dialogue with all its participants, since the process of city making requires 20% imagination and 80% communication!

Bangkok — Street Food: A Common Canteen

Urban Design and Development Centre (UddC) aims to be a deliberative platform to engage a wide range of stakeholders in the city. It includes local government, the public and private sectors and civil society in a decision-making process in order to propose innovative solutions for urban development. UddC provides consultancy services and urban planning and design in parallel with experimental research.

The GoodWalk Thailand Project is a research and development endeavor to create an open database, the first of its kind in Thailand. The first part of this research is the study of urban morphology, which has been converted into an Accessibility Index. Further studies on the distribution of public amenities for pedestrian-friendly urban locations are then converted into a Walkability Index. The research findings are disseminated to the public via a web platform and interactive map at www.goodwalk.org.

Barcelona — Mixed Use, Mixed Time, Mixed People

The metropolitan area of Barcelona is a territorial, social, demographic, economic, and cultural fact formed over the last century; it is a product of the growth and connection of urban systems around the city. It covers 636 square kilometers with more than 3.2 million inhabitants organized in thirty-six municipalities. AMB (Barcelona Metropolitan Area) is the public administration that manages this territory.

The Institute for Advanced Architecture of Catalonia (IAAC) is an experimental and experiential center for research, education, production, and outreach, with the mission of envisioning the future habitat and building it in the present. It is inspired by the values of Barcelona, the capital of architecture and design, where urbanism was invented.

Beijing — Code City

Code City is a research initiative launched by Yungho Chang and Zheng Tan in the Department of Architecture at Tongji University. So far, a series of graduate studios, charrettes, symposia, and lectures has been organized at Tongji University to unearth the secret life of code-making in Chinese cities. This project received support from the College of Architecture and Urban Planning at Tongji University, Time+Architecture Journal, and the Let's Talk Forum.

Berlin — *Die Laube* in the City Garden: Architecture as a Trigger Towards a Co-produced City

Christian Burkhard is an economist by training. After his studies at the University of Economics in Vienna and at the London School of Economics, where he also read philosophy, he worked in France as a consultant for the public and private sector. Since 2013, Burkhard has been collaborating with Florian Köhl.

Florian Köhl is a German architect. After his studies at the Technical University, Munich and the Bartlett School of Architecture, London, where he also was a Unit Master, he taught from 2000 to 2006 at the Technical University, Berlin. In 2002, he founded his own practice, fatkoehl architects. In 2009, Köhl won the Berlin Architecture Award. In 2015, he was nominated for the Mies van der Rohe Award for European Architecture.

Changwon — Three Cities: Assemblage Urbanism

Professor Jin Seok Park completed his studies in 2002 at AA in the U.K, after which he worked on key urban regeneration projects in London including Coin Street and Kidbrooke Regeneration project, and founded Phos Architects, in collaboration with urbanists and architects, and delivered Nalut University project in Libya. Since joining School of Architecture at Kyungnam University as an assistant professor in 2013, he has worked on a number of regeneration projects including Regeneration Strategy and Co-op Social Housing for Changwon, and also organised International Environment Conference for Sustainable City. He is also Unit Master of AA Visiting School Seoul since 2014.

Chennai — At the Cross-Rivers: Reconnecting Chennai

Raghuram Avula is the founder and director of Studio RDA Chennai, a strategic design consultancy with a multidisciplinary approach, where architecture plays a key role in conceptualization and problem solving. He has been studying the changing urban identity of Chennai to develop sustainable ideas.

He received his degree in architecture from the School of Architecture and Planning, Anna University, Chennai, in 1996 and was visiting faculty there from 2004 to 2009. He has designed many exhibitions for the InKo Centre, Crafts Council of India. British Council, and the recent pavilion at the K Art International Art Fair held at Busan in 2016. *At Cross-Rivers: Reconnecting Chennai* is presented by the InKo Centre, Chennai, in association with the School of Architecture and Planning, Anna University, Chennai.

Chinese Cities — Ghost Cities: Understanding Patterns in Chinese Urbanization

The Civic Data Design Lab works with data, maps, and mobile technologies to develop interactive design and communication strategies that bring urban policy issues to broader audiences. The lab experiments with data visualization and data collection tools to achieve results that are more relevant and more responsive to the needs and interests of citizens, traditionally on the margins of policy development.

Dubai — Projected Futures for the Commons in Dubai

George Katodrytis is Professor of Architecture and Head of the Department of Architecture in the College of Architecture, Art and Design at the American University of Sharjah.

Mi Chang has studied engineering and has worked in Seoul and Dubai as a project manager and consultant. She is a member of the team advising on cultural and urban issues.

Maryam Mudhaffar is an architect and architectural historian, currently working as a Senior Rehabilitation Engineer at the Architectural Heritage and Antiquities Department of the Dubai Municipality.

Kevin Mitchell is Professor of Architecture in the College of Architecture, Art and Design and Vice Provost of Undergraduate Affairs and Instruction at the American University of Sharjah.

EM/MENA — Connecting Cities: Commonalities and Challenges

Originally from the island of Cyprus, Melina Nicolaides was born in Washington, D.C., and grew up in Asia and Europe. She holds a BA in History from Princeton University and an MFA from the Maryland Institute College of Art, which she attended as an A.G. Leventis scholar. As a visual artist, her work has been shown in more than fifty exhibitions internationally. At present, her focus is creating cross-disciplinary projects that address pressing environmental, social, and political issues of the Eastern Mediterranean/Middle East-North Africa area. These ongoing initiatives endeavor to bring together people from across this region and from diverse fields of knowledge to build solution-oriented collaborations.

Future Earth is a major international research platform with central hubs and regional centers across the globe. It aims to provide the knowledge and support to accelerate transformations to a sustainable world, including scientific projects that work across the natural and social sciences on critical global change and sustainability issues. The Future Earth MENA Regional Center (FEMRC) serves countries in the Eastern Mediterranean, the Middle East, and North Africa and enables initiatives that cater to the specific characteristics of the region and its pressing environmental and societal challenges. Its goal is to foster regionally coordinated research and the implementation of strategies that develop sustainable lifestyles and economies.

Nicosia — Climate Change Hot Spot: Future's Extremes

Created in 2005, the Cyprus Institute is a nonprofit research and post-graduate education institution with a strong scientific and technological orientation. Its research is conducted in three cross-disciplinary centers, which address challenging problems that are important in the Eastern Mediterranean and Middle East-North Africa region as well as at the international level, through an interdisciplinary, integrative approach. An essential element of the Institute's mission is to develop recommendations for effective and comprehensive adaptation strategies that will contribute to the sustainable development of the region's countries and societies.

Athens — From Antiquity to Tomorrow: The People's Water Project

EYDAP is the Water Supply & Sewerage Company of the greater metropolitan area of Athens and the district of Attica. It is the largest water and wastewater management company in Greece and reaches nearly six million people, who are supplied with potable water by a distribution network made up of over 9,500 kilometers of water pipeline. EYDAP also designs, manages, and maintains infrastructure, upgrades water systems, and upholds quality control. The environmental protection policy of EYDAP aims to ensure the sustainable management of this important resource and the preservation of ecosystem equilibrium in the natural environment of Greece.

Alexandria — After Past and Present: Determining the Future

The Bibliotheca Alexandrina was rebuilt in 2002 to commemorate the original Library of Alexandria, the largest and most significant library of the ancient world. As a symbol of culture and knowledge, the Bibliotheca is dedicated to recapturing the spirit of openness and scholarship of its ancient namesake. Continuing its historical engagement with the city and its residents, this institution is also a vast complex where arts, history, philosophy, and science come together. It not only maintains Ptolemy I's collection from 300 BCE, it also houses a vast Main Library, specialized libraries for rare books and maps, ten academic research centers, museums and temporary exhibitions galleries, a conference center, a planetarium, and a manuscript restoration laboratory.

Gwangju — Cultural Landscape of the City: Gwangju Folly

Hong-guen Park, an architect, participated in Gwangju Folly I as a local artist with two works: *99Kan* [99 Rooms] and *Public Room*. He is currently the Chair of the Gwangju/South Jeolla Province Chapter of the Korean Institute of Architects (KIA). He is also an architectural and cultural activist. Since 1995, he has been the principal of For You Architects. He writes columns on current issues relevant to urban architectural issues.

The Gwangju Biennale Foundation has been in charge of organizing the Gwangju Biennale since 1995. *Gwangju Folly* began in 2011 as part of the Gwangju Design Biennale; since 2013, the *Folly* has become an independent project.

Hong Kong / Shenzhen — By-City / By-Product

Peter W. Ferretto graduated from both Cambridge and Liverpool Universities. He worked as a registered architect (ARB) for several international architectural practices, including Herzog & de Meuron, before establishing, PWFERRETTO in 2009. Since 2014, he has taught at the Chinese University of Hong Kong as Associate Professor of Design and Practice.

Doreen Heng Liu received her M.Arch from UC Berkeley and her Doctor of Design from the Harvard Graduate School of Design. Her research focuses on contemporary urbanism and architecture in the Pearl River Delta and the specific impact of urbanization on design and practice in China today. Since 2011, she has taught at the Chinese University of Hong Kong as Associate Adjunct Professor of Urban Design and Practice.

Jakarta — Micro Practice and Macro Perspective for Building Resilience in an Urban *Kampung*

Since 2011, Megacity Design Lab, a laboratory of international collaboration between Japan and Indonesia, has worked to re-evaluate our ways of living. Our current practice, in one of the most densely populated areas in Jakarta, addresses our increasing concern over limited resources as well as the rapidly growing population by putting architectural and urban design practices within the community. In this exhibition, we attempt to illustrate an alternate perspective that sees densely populated areas as an alternative way of living, and to celebrate the urban commons that are revealed within communities.

Jeju — *Dolchanggo*: Between Home and Nomadism, Jeju Rurbanism

The exhibition on Jeju was organized with the active participation and support of the Jeju Branch of the Korea Institute of Registered Architects. A seven member team of architects, artists, photographers, and designers came together through the Institute to plan and install the exhibition. The Korea Institute of Registered Architects, Jeju Branch, has a membership of about 270 architects on Jeju Island. "Jeju phenomenon," the theme of the exhibition, was also the title of a book, supplementary to the main book celebrating 50 years of architecture on Jeju. (The authors of the supplementary book are Gwang-su Kim, Jae-won Jo, and Seung-hoe Gu.) The organizers of the exhibition received advice and assistance from the authors and the editors of the supplementary book.

The four architects are Seongcheon Go, YANG Geon, HONG Gwang-taek, and HYEON Gi-wook. Go led the architect team. GANG Jeong-hyo was in charge of Jeju-related photographs; NOH Gyeon was in charge of architecture-related photographs; and Prof. YI In-ho of Jeju International University was in charge of design and editing. The government of Jeju Special Self-Governing Province also participated in this exhibition as co-organizers.

Johannesburg — Shifting Borders and Building Bridges

The Gauteng City-Region is South Africa's economic heartland and includes the cities of Johannesburg and Pretoria. It holds thirteen million people and generates a third of South Africa's GDP, on 1.5% of its land area. The Gauteng City-Region Observatory (GCRO) builds the data and analysis to help inform development in this region.

London — London Made

Working in partnership, the Mayor of London, the British Council, New London Architecture, and SEGRO, have appointed We Made That to curate London's exhibition. We Made That is an energetic architecture and urbanism practice with a strong public conscience. The practice works with public sector clients to prepare and deliver incisive urban research, responsive area strategies and master plans, and distinctive architecture and public realm projects. We Made That has been working closely with public and local authorities on a number of research projects and strategies that explore the city's relationship with industry and production.

London, Annex — Place, Spaces, Work

Publica is a London-based research and urban design agency that advises local authorities, landowners, developers, architects and community organisations. Publica's extensive fieldwork and research on urban neighbourhoods has been sought out by international city planners and public authorities. The Store Studios, 180 The Strand is a unique creative space and complex of broadcast studios housed in an iconic Brutalist building in central London. It hosts high profile exhibitions, houses a mix of creative media companies, and is the new home of London Fashion Week.

Macao — Macao Shaped by Use: Formalizing the Vernacular Customization of the City

Based in Macao since 2003, Nuno Soares is an architect and urban planner who spreads his practice through architectural design, teaching, and research. He is the principal of his own office, URBAN PRACTICE, teaches in Macao at USJ and at the Chinese University of Hong Kong, and is the Vice President of Arcasia Zone C. He founded and directs the CURB (Center for Architecture and Urbanism), a nonprofit organization created in Macao to promote the research, education, production, and diffusion of knowledge in the fields of architecture, urbanism, design, and urban culture. CURB acts both on a regional level and internationally, taking local issues to a global audience, and acting as a think-tank on the future of cities and their architecture.

Madrid — DREAMadrid

Dr. José Luis Esteban Penelas is an architect and chaired Professor at the School of Architecture, European University of Madrid (UEM). In 1992, he established his own office of Architecture and Urbanism in Madrid; Penelas Architects is a creative office of architecture, urban design, and infrastructural design and is one of the most renowned architectural practices in Spain. His projects and works have been internationally published; he has received more than fifty national and international awards, and his works have been exhibited worldwide. He is also the founder and director of the Research Group: AIR LAB CITIES (Advanced Architecture International Research Laboratory of Cities).

Medellín — A City for Life

Curator and manager of the exhibit, architect Jorge Pérez-Jaramillo, was Dean of the Facultad de Arquitectura Universidad Pontificia Bolivariana (UPB), Medellín, Colombia, from 1993 to 2001. He practiced as an architect and planner from 1987 to 2016, and was City Planning Director of Medellín from 2012 to 2015. He served as coordinator of the Lee Kuan Yew World City Prize, Medellín, in 2016, and of the Special Mention 2014 awards. In 2017, he was appointed a visiting fellow at King's College, Cambridge; he is currently writing about Medellín's urban evolution.

Co-curator of design and production, Sebastián Monsalve-Gómez, is an architect based in Medellín. He was a project designer and competition winner for Medellín River Parks, Civic Hall, and Nutibara Hill Master Plans in 2013 to 2017, and he is currently a partner at Latitud taller.

Messina — Messina Waterfront Polycenter: A Socio-Economic and Cultural Catalyst

Founded in London in 1996, Urban Future Organization seeks to address the issues relating to the development of urbanity and architecture within contemporary culture. The organization operates as a network of independent architectural offices, each office responding to its own locale whilst being able to draw on the resources of a global collective. To date, this includes offices in UK, Greece, Italy, Netherlands, Australia, South Korea, China, Turkey, USA, Sweden, Saudi Arabia, Indonesia. Its members are multinational design professionals, who conduct their work through collaboration with experienced consultants. Urban future organization has professional backgrounds ranging from the execution of a single residential house to national concert hall.

Mexico City — A Living Laboratory to Prototype: The Future of the Cities We Want

Laboratorio para la Ciudad is the experimental arm/creative think-tank of the government of Mexico City; it reports to the mayor. Working across such diverse areas as urban creativity, mobility, governance, civic tech, and public space, the Lab is a place to reflect about all things city and to explore other social scripts and urban futures for the largest megalopolis in the Western hemisphere. In addition, the Lab seeks to create links between civil society and government, constantly shifting shape to accommodate multidisciplinary collaborations, insisting on the importance of political and public imagination in the execution of its experiments.

Mumbai — The Bench-Ladder Conversations: Between Systems and Madness

BARD Studio is a joint initiative of Rupali Gupte and Prasad Shetty, who are both urbanists. They teach at the School of Environment and Architecture in Mumbai, an experimental academic space they co-founded along with six other architects. They had also co-founded an urban research network, CRIT. In their conceptualization, cities are incoherent, unbound, and unstable and get worked out through multiple messy logics. Their works take different forms: writings, drawings, mixed-media works, storytelling, teaching, walks, and spatial interventions. Their works have been shown at Manifesta, Bolzano, 2008; Audi Urban Future Award, Istanbul, 2012; São Paulo Architecture Biennale, 2013; and at the Venice Art Biennale, 2015.

Oslo — Edible Oslo

Transborder Studio is an architecture office founded by Øystein Rø and Espen Røyseland, based in Oslo, Norway. Transborder Studio makes architecture, urbanism, and landscapes of all scales, including plans for the new city integrated agricultural district—a center for urban farming in Oslo.

Soyoung Lee is botanist and a botanical illustrator based in Seoul, Korea.

Paris — *Réinventer* Paris

Created in 1988, Pavillon de l'Arsenal, Center for Architecture and Urban Planning of Paris and Parisian metropolis, is a unique place where the arrangement of the city and its architectural realizations are put within the reach of all. The key missions of the Pavillon de l'Arsenal are to explain the "architecture" of the city, its development over the centuries, its present state and prospects for the future as well as to present the urban expertise of Paris, its architects and contractors to foreign visitors. Located in the heart of Paris, the Pavillon de l'Arsenal presents each year more than 15 exhibitions in France and abroad.

Pyongyang — Pyongyang Sallim

Dongwoo Yim is the co-founder of

PRAUD and an Assistant Professor at Hongik University. He received his master's degree at Harvard University and his bachelor's degree at Seoul National University. He was the winner of the Architectural League Prize in 2013 and is the author of "Pyongyang, and Pyongyang After," "(Un) Precedented Pyongyang," and "North Korean Atlas," among other works. His works have been exhibited in the award-winning Korean Pavilion at the Venice Biennale in 2014, at the Museum of Modern Art in New York, and at DNA Galerie in Berlin. He was previously an Adjunct Professor at the Rhode Island School of Design and a visiting assistant professor at Washington University in St. Louis.

Calvin Chua is the founder of Spatial Anatomy and is an Adjunct Assistant Professor at the Singapore University of Technology and Design (SUTD). At the same time, Calvin directs an architectural workshop in Pyongyang through the AA Visiting School Programme and Choson Exchange, which has been featured in various news media. An alumnus of the Architectural Association in London, Calvin is a registered architect in the United Kingdom.

Reykjavík — The Hot Pot as Political Arena

Arna Mathiesen is one of two founding partners of April Arkitekter AS, an architectural practice and research unit based in Oslo, Norway, with projects ranging from furniture to large housing estates and urban developments on the fringe of Europe. Mathiesen is originally from Iceland. She holds a BA (Hons) in architecture from Kingston Polytechnic in the United Kingdom and graduated with an MArch degree from Princeton University in 1996.

Rome — The Theaters of Culture: Ephemeral Projects for the Eternal City

Architect, critic, and professor, Pippo Ciorra, contributes to journals, reviews, and the national press, and is author of many essays and publications. He was a member of the editorial board of *Casabella* from 1996 to 2012 and is the author of a number of books, including monographic studies on Quaroni, Eisenman, museums, the city, photography, and contemporary Italian architecture. He teaches design and theory at SAAD (University of Camerino) and is the director of the international PhD program Villard d'Honnecourt (IUAV). In 2016, he was part of the jury for the XV Architecture Biennale in Venice. He has curated and designed exhibitions in Italy and abroad. Since 2009, he has been Senior Curator of MAXXI Architettura in Rome. Among his major exhibitions are Re-cycle, Energy, Food and The Japanese House. He curates the Italian branch of YAP, the MoMA PS1 international program for young architects.

San Diego / Tijuana

See "Tijuana / San Diego"

San Francisco — At Home Together

The Urban Works Agency (UWA), directed by Neeraj Bhatia and Antje Steinmuller, is a design-research lab at the California College of the Arts (CCA). UWA focuses on how to leverage architectural design to effect social justice, ecological vitality, and economic resilience at the urban scale.

Neeraj Bhatia is a licensed architect and urban designer whose work resides at the intersection of politics, infrastructure, and urbanism. He is an Assistant Professor at CCA and founder of a design practice, The Open Workshop. Antje Steinmuller is an Assistant Professor at CCA, principal at the architecture practice Studio Urbis, and cofounder of ideal X, a design consultancy focused on the conditions and opportunities of public spaces in transition.

São Paulo — Food Circuit in São Paulo

Denise Xavier de Mendonça is an architect with a master's degree in the theory and history of architecture from the Institute of Architecture and Urbanism of the University of São Paulo. She is a Professor at the Centro Universitário de Belas Artes de São Paulo and the author of the book *Arquitetura Metropolitana, São Paulo* (Annblume, 2007).

Anderson Kazuo Nakano is an architect and urban planner with a master's degree in environmental and urban structures and a PhD in demography. He was the coordinator of the last review of São Paulo's Strategic Master Plan, and he is a Professor at the Centro Universitário de Belas Artes de São Paulo.

Sejong — Zero-Energy Smart City Development

The National Agency for Administrative City Construction (NAACC) is the government agency responsible for the construction of the "administrative city," now called Sejong City. Launched in 2006, the agency has been responsible for planning, managing and attracting investment for the construction of Sejong, an integrated city with a concentration of government administrative buildings. The city was newly developed specifically to relocate a large segment of the Korean national government, the offices of which were traditionally concentrated in Seoul and its environs. The goal of the government relocation was a nationwide "balanced development" and a reduction of overpopulation in the larger metropolitan Seoul area. NAACC is proud of the historical mission it has been appointed to carry out and we are doing our utmost to make sure that the new city becomes "a global benchmark city that everyone wishes to live in."

Korea Land and Housing Corporation is a public corporation established to promote the improvement of housing and the efficient use of national land. Its duties include the acquisition, development, banking, and supply of land; urban development and maintenance; and the construction, supply, and management of housing. By supplying 2.6 million units of public housing, the corporation has contributed to securing housing stability for the working poor. In addition, by developing new cities around the nation, it has developed land and expanded social overhead capital such as roads and schools, and thus contributed to the growth of the national economy. The corporation undertakes the construction of the administrative city. As such, it exerts efforts to make sure that the new city will be representative of innovative urban planning, not only in Korea, but also globally.

Seoul — Sectioning Seoul

As an architect and educator, Sora Kim is currently a faculty member at the University of Seoul (Department of Architecture, School of Architecture and Architectural Engineering). She received her MA in Architecture from the University of Pennsylvania and is a New York Registered Architect with work experience in New York and New Jersey.

She is also active as a Seoul Public Architect and as the head of Park and Kim Architects. For her work on the Daeeun Elementary School Student Lounge, she was selected as a finalist for the Architizer 2013 A+ Awards. In 2015, for Hwigyeong Children's Library, she received an architecture award from the Korean Institute of Culture Architecture [sic], as well as a letter of citation from the head of the Dongdaemun borough, or *gu*. In 2012, she received a letter of citation from the Minister of Culture, Sports and Tourism for her contribution to architecture and culture.

Seoul, Seongbuk — Seongbuk Art Commons

Seongbuk Art Commons was planned and organized jointly by Seongbuk Cultural Foundation (Young Art Space) and Co-op Art Plug. The members of the joint planning group are as follows: Kim Nan-yeong, Kim Mi-jeong, Kim Wung-gi, Kim Jin-man, Yi Hyeon, Jang Yu-jung, and Hong Jang-o.

Seongbuk Cultural Foundation is engaged in producing cultural and artistic content that utilizes a variety of cultural-historical resources available in the neighborhood; it supports strong relationships and coordination between artists, on the one hand, and local business owners and residents on the other. Its aim is to build a stronger community, cultural democracy, and a cultural-artistic ecosystem through these efforts.

Young Art Space is one of the institutions run by Seongbuk Cultural Foundation. It organizes exhibitions and projects and promotes networking among artists. It serves as the art and culture platform of the Seongbuk area. One of its ongoing projects is the archiving and visualization of the various neighborhood resources, both natural and cultural.

Co-op Art Plug is an artist cooperative whose membership includes visual and other artists. It promotes and presents sustainable and stable artistic and cultural programs practiced in close understanding of and connection with the local community. To do so, it has been building a government-grassroots cooperative network; its aim is to activate a cultural and artistic ecosystem in the Seongbuk area.

SH Corporation — Seoul Housing and Community Movements 1: Towards Open Communities

Jieun Kim received her Ph.D in Urban Planning and Policy from the University of Illinois at Chicago. She is currently conducts research into urban regeneration and housing policy at the Urban Research Institute of Seoul Housing and Communities Corporation.

Tae-jin Lee and Gyeong Oh Chung (05Studio) are a young architect group based in Seoul. They studied at Delft University of Technology and have worked in the Netherlands and Singapore. Based on their work experiences, they are currently engaged in various urban and architectural experiments.

Seoul Housing and Communities Corporation is a public corporation established in 1989 with funding from the Seoul Metropolitan Government. Through residential land development and provision, as well as management of public housing, it has contributed to housing stability and improved the quality of life for the homeless in Seoul. Since 2015, the corporation has proclaimed itself as an urban regeneration and housing welfare corporation; it changed its name from its previous Seoul Housing Corporation to its current Seoul Housing and Communities Corporation. The Korean name of the corporation, *Seoul jutaek dosi gongsa* (Seoul housing and urban corporation) emphasizes the role of the corporation as a public developer that creates jobs and solves urban problems at large, beyond the scope of solving Seoul's housing problems. The English name "Seoul Housing and Communities Corporation" reflects its orientation, which is to address the issues of housing and building communities simultaneously.

SH Corporation — Seoul Housing and Community Movements 2: Landscripts for New Communities: Seoul via Vienna

A teaching and practicing architect in Vienna, Austria, Mladen Jadric is the founder and principal of JADRIC ARCHITEKTUR ZT GmbH. He has realized a wide range of projects at different scales: architectural and urban design projects, including residences, experimental art installations, and interior design in Austria, the United States, Finland, and China. Since 1997, he has been an Assistant Professor at the Vienna University of Technology and has gained extensive experience as a visiting professor and guest lecturer in Europe, USA, Asia, Australia, and South America. He has exhibited at the Royal Academy of Arts in London; MIT, Cooper Union, and Roger Williams University in the United States; Alvar Aalto University in Helsinki, Finland; the Architectural Biennale in Venice, Italy; the World Architectural Triennale in Tokyo, Japan; the Museum of the 20th Century in Berlin, Germany; BUGAIK International Architecture Exhibition in Busan, Korea; NIT-Nagoya Institute of Technology in Japan, and many more. He has received the State Award for Experimental Architecture, Karl Scheffel Preis and Schorsch Preis from the City of Vienna.

Hae-Won Shin is the founder of lokaldesign. She has realized a wide range of projects differing in scale, ranging from infrastructure across the Han River, to large and small public projects, to interiors and cardboard chair design. She is currently a Projects Director at Publica where she leads a number of projects, including the detailed design of the public realm, infrastructure, and master planning context in an expansive area of West London, and a vision for the Oxford Street District. She has been an Assistant Professor at the Chinese University of Hong Kong and the Korea National University of Arts. She has exhibited at the Cass Bank, 2015; Venice Architecture Biennale, 2006; Aedes Gallery, Berlin; the MAK, Vienna, and RMIT Design Hub in Melbourne. In 2013, she was awarded the Young Architect Award and Public Design Awards in Korea.

Shanghai — The Other Factory: Late-Industrial Organization and Form

This investigation and exhibition is the result of a collaboration between SKEW Collaborative and the University of Hong Kong, led by H. Koon Wee, Darren Zhou, Eunice Seng, and Lam Lai Shun. The specificity of this late-industrial period of development in China emerged from a decade of award-winning architectural and urban projects designed by SKEW Collaborative. It has led to analyses of how the architecture of industry presents itself as an organizational and urban complex. This project is supported by a HKU research grant looking closely at the Sino-Soviet period. SKEW Collaborative is an architectural and research practice currently based in Shanghai and Hong Kong. Its principals and associates are also faculty members and researchers at HKU, where they connect with a broader teaching agenda under the auspices of the Cities in Asia Summer Program.

Shenzhen — Shenzhen to PRD Method

FUTURE + Aformal Academy is an independent academy for urbanism, landscape, and public art in China. Our pedagogy emerges from the open innovation ecosystems of Shenzhen. The methodology of the PRD means designs and the city are created, tested, and evolved quickly. Traditional urbanism was about order; we embrace the unpredictable and the messy. This allows us to form a place for rapid response urban learning. We mine the gaps of the city to identify integral points for action. Our focus is not to instill a dogma but to facilitate individuals' learning ambitions. FUTURE + is a hybrid research institute, think-tank, and experimental laboratory. We have been formed by many of the same folks that set up and run the Shenzhen/Hong Kong Urbanism/Architecture Biennale and the Shenzhen Center for Design.

Singapore — White Space

The Singapore University of Technology and Design (SUTD) is Singapore's fourth public university and one of the first universities in the world to incorporate the art and science of design and technology into a multidisciplinary curriculum. SUTD was established in collaboration with the Massachusetts Institute of Technology and seeks to advance knowledge and nurture technically grounded leaders and innovators to serve societal needs.

In collaboration with Zhejiang University, SUTD, a research-intensive university, is distinguished by its unique East and West academic programs, which incorporate elements of entrepreneurship, management, and design thinking. SUTD offers four pillars of study: Architecture and Sustainable Design (ASD), Engineering Product Development, Engineering Systems and Design, and Information Systems Technology and Design. ASD prepares students for the future needs of architecture in a digital era: ecological urban architecture, leveraging big data to design smart cities, advanced design computation, digital fabrication, and more.

Sydney — Spatial Frameworks: City Strategy in the Twenty-first Century

Professor Gerard Reinmuth is a Founding Director of the architectural firm TERROIR and is Professor of Practice in the School of Architecture at the University of Technology, Sydney. TERROIR has been featured in numerous international publications, biennales, and awards programs for its built work, while Reinmuth's research and teaching explore the agency of the architect, given contemporary economic and political tendencies. This work has culminated in Reinmuth's current research project, "Towards a Relational Architecture" (in collaboration with Professor Andrew Benjamin) which, in re-thinking the discipline, might inform a new conception of the profession.

Tehran — Cultivating Tehran

Established in 2016, Tehran Urban Innovation Center (TUIC) is a design-by-research, research-by-design practice, dedicated to developing ideas for smart urban solutions for contemporary Iranian cities. The center aims to tackle pressing urban issues through deployment of novel technologies with the ultimate goal of making existing Iranian cities smarter, more resilient, and as sustainable as possible.

Amin Tadjsoleiman Amin received his master's degree in architecture from the Faculty of Fine Arts at the University of Tehran. He is the co-founder of VAVStudio in Iran, through which he has designed and executed several institutional, commercial, and residential projects during the last fourteen years. VAVStudio's projects have earned several national and international awards and recognition, and have been displayed in several exhibitions including the Venice Biennale, 2016.

Tijuana / San Diego — Living Borders

Rene Peralta is a Lecturer in the Art and Design program at San Diego State University. He is co-author, with anthropologist Fiamma Montezemolo and writer Heriberto Yepez, of the book *Here is Tijuana* (London: Black Dog Publishing, 2006). From 2012 to 2014, he was the Director of the Master of Science in Architecture with emphasis on Landscape + Urbanism at Woodbury University School of Architecture in San Diego. In 2015, his work on PREVI in Lima, Peru, was part of the exhibit *Latin America in Construction: Architecture 1955–1980* at the Museum of Modern Art in New York. Currently, he forms part of Hyperloop West, one of the eleven United States semi-finalist teams developing a hyperloop transportation route from Los Angeles to Ensenada, Mexico.

Tokyo — Common Matters

Co-curator Christian Dimmer is an Assistant Professor at Waseda University School of International Liberal Studies. Dimmer graduated from the Technical University of Kaierslautern, Germany, and earned his PhD from the University of Tokyo. He is co-founder of the design-led disaster response organization, Architecture for Humanity, Tokyo chapter, as well as of the TPF²/Tohoku Planning Forum.

Co-curator Keigo Kobayashi is an architect and Associate Professor in the Department of Architecture at Waseda University in Tokyo. He graduated from the Harvard Graduate School of Design in 2005, and worked at OMA/AMO in Rotterdam until 2012. Since then, he has been teaching design and leading a lab at Waseda University. In 2017, he also co-founded the Network of Research & Architecture (NoRA), based in Amsterdam.

Vienna — The Vienna Model

Wolfgang Förster, PhD, has studied architecture, planning, and political science in Vienna and Graz, and has worked as an architect and researcher. He was Deputy Director of the Vienna Housing Fund, and from 1991 until 2001, he was Head of Vienna Housing Research. He is an Austrian Delegate to the UNECE Committee on Housing and Land Management and has been Chair of this Committee since 2009. In 2015, he received the Golden Honorary Medal for Achievements from the Federal State of Vienna.

Förster is author of numerous publications on public housing and urban renewal. He is currently the coordinator of IBA-Vienna (the 2020–2022 international building exhibition on *New Social Housing*), and he works at his own company PUSH-Consulting (Partners on Urbanism and Sustainable Housing).

Yeongju — Multiple Systems of Urban-Rural Integrated City: Yeongju's Public Architecture Masterplan

In 2009, Yeongju City was the first local government ever in Korea to designate, in accordance with the Framework Act on Building, civilian experts on architecture and urbanism. The two experts who were initially appointed were "public architects," and they provided advice on the city's public architectural projects. After this initial experiment, it was agreed by all parties involved—that is, the city employees as well as the civilian experts—that a coordinator and a team dedicated to supervising and coordinating the city's public architecture programs were needed. Thus, in 2010, the city appointed another public architect and established the Design Management Team. Currently, Yeongju City operates a two-tier system. The head of the Design Management Team oversees public architecture and related projects at the city-wide level; at the same time, the city also operates the Yeongju City Public Architect program where designated public architects are responsible for supervising individual city projects.

Cityscape — Homo Urbanus

Video artists Bêka & Lemoine have been working together for the past ten years focusing their research on experimental new narrative and cinematographic forms in relation to contemporary architecture and the urban environment. Since their first film *Koolhaas Houselife* (2008), internationally renowned as an "architecture cult movie" (*El Pais*), they have been developing a film series widely acclaimed as "a new form of criticism" (*Mark*), that "has deeply changed the way of looking at architecture" (*Domus*). Selected as one of the hundred most talented personalities of 2017 by Icon Design, Bêka & Lemoine were named by the Metropolitan Museum of Art in New York as one of the "most exciting and critical design projects of the year 2016." The complete work of Bêka & Lemoine has been acquired by the Museum of Modern Art in New York for their permanent collection.

Toward a (Dis)-Educating City: The (Dis)-Educational Workshop

Giuseppe Stampone is an artist based in Rome and Brussels. He continuously endeavors to introduce an alternative social-political agenda through his art works and community-based interventions. His works engage audiences to mediate on basic issues such as immigration, water, and war. Stampone founded the network Solstizio, co-financed by the European Union, and works with diverse groups of artists, universities, museums, NGOs, and public institutions. In 2013, he was awarded a fellowship at the American Academy in Rome, and also won the Art Residency at Young Eun Museum of Contemporary Art (YMCA) in Gwangju, South Korea. His work has been exhibited in international art biennials, museums, and foundations including the Venice Biennial, 2015; the Kochi-Muziris Biennial, 2012; the Havana Biennial, 2012; the Liverpool Biennial, 2010; and many others.

Curator: Helen Hejung Choi
Associate Curator: Hyoeun Kim
Associate Curator: Donghwa Kang
Assistant Curator: Dasom Gong
Project Manager: Ri Jin Yoo

Exhibition Space Design: OBRA Architects
Exhibition Design Manager: Jina Lee

History of City Planning — From the "Functional City" to "Total Function": Planning the Modern City, 1925–1971

Curators: Annie Pedret
Participants & Affiliations: Het Nieuwe Instituut, Tange Associates, Kyu Sung Woo

Cities in Comparison — Dynamics of the Urban Age

Curators: Ricky Burdett, Aron Bohmann, Peter Griffiths
Participants & Affiliations: Emily Cruz (LSE Cities, Project Coordinator), Alfred Herrhausen Gesellschaft (AHG)

Future of Cities — Humanity, Cities, and the Environment

Curators: National Geographic
Participants & Affiliations: Seoyeon Park, Sohwa Ahn, Mimi Kim

Amsterdam — Amsterdam Approach

Curators: Eric van der Burg, Eric van der Kooij
Participants & Affiliations: Esther Agricola, City of Amsterdam Department of Planning and Sustainability

Bangkok — Street Food: A Common Canteen

Curators: Niramon Kulsrisombat
Participants & Affiliations: Urban Design Development Center (UddC), Piya Limpiti (Assistant Curator/Designer)

Barcelona — Mixed Use, Mixed Time, Mixed People

Curators: Vicente Guallart
Participants & Affiliations: Barcelona Metropolitan Area (AMB), Institute for Advanced Architecture of Catalonia (IAAC), Ramon Torra (Coordinator)

Beijing — Code City

Curators: Zheng Tan, Yung Ho Chang
Participants & Affiliations: Code City Research Team, Tongji University,

Yemo Li (Assistsant Curator), Time+Archictecture Journal

Berlin — *Die Laube* in the City Garden: Architecture as a Trigger Towards a Co-produced City
Curators: Christian Burkhard, Florian Kohl (Quest | An Urban Laboratory)
Participants & Affiliations: Deutsche Bundesstiftung Umwelt, Marco Clausen (Contents Design), Philipp Misselwitz (Research)

Changwon — Three Cities: Assemblage Urbanism
Curators: Jin Seok Park
Participants & Affiliations: Changwon City, Changwon Institute of Registered Architects, Changwon Regeneration Center

Chennai — At the Cross-Rivers: Reconnecting Chennai
Curators: Raghuram Avula
Participants & Affiliations: InKo Centre, Dr. Rathi Jafer (Director), School of Architecture and Planning, Anna University Chennai

Chinese Cities — Ghost Cities: Understanding Patterns in Chinese Urbanization
Curators: Sarah Williams
Participants & Affiliations: Civic Data Design Lab, MIT, Massachusetts Institute Technology Department of Urban Studies Planning (DUSP), Chaewon Ahn (Exhibition Design/Construction)

Dubai — Projected Futures for the Commons in Dubai
Curators: George Katodrytis, Kevin Mitchell, Maryam Mudhaffar, Mi Chang

EM/MENA — Connecting Cities: Commonalities and Challenges
Curators: Melina Nicolaides
Participants & Affiliations: Future Earth MENA Regional Center, The Cyprus Institute's 'Energy, Environment and Water Research Center' (EEWRC), Manfred A. Lange, Georgios Artopoulos (Research Material, Scientific Data, Design)

Nicosia — Climate Change Hot Spot: Future's Extremes
Curators: Melina Nicolaides
Participants & Affiliations: The Cyprus Institute's 'Science & Technology in Archaeology Research Center' (STARC),

'Computation-based Science and Technology Research Center' (CaSToRC), Manfred A. Lange, Georgios Artopoulos (Research Material, Scientific Data, Design)

Athens — From Antiquity to Tomorrow: The People's Water Project
Curators: Melina Nicolaides
Participants & Affiliations: EYDAP, the Water Supply & Sewerage Company of the Greater Metropolitan Area of Athens, Lambrini Tzamourani (Production), Eftihia Nestoridou (Production), Giorgos Sachinis (Production), Sonia Tzimopoulou (Production)

Alexandria — After Past and Present: Determining the Future
Curators: Melina Nicolaides
Participants & Affiliations: The 'Alexandria and Mediterranean Research Center', The 'Center for Sustainable Development Studies' of the Bibliotheca Alexandrina, Salah A. Soliman

Gwangju — Cultural Landscape of the City: Gwangju Folly
Curators: Hong-guen Park, Gwangju Biennale
Participants & Affiliations: Gwangju Division TOINAD Co., Ltd., Studio Kerb

Hong Kong/Shenzhen — By-City/By-Product
Curators: Peter Ferretto, Doreen Liu
Participants & Affiliations: The Chinese University of Hong Kong

Jakarta — Micro Practice and Macro Perspective for Building Resilience in an Urban *Kampung*
Curators: Megacity Design Lab

Jeju — *Dolchanggo*: Between Home and Nomadism, Jeju Rurbanism
Curators: Korea Institute of Registered Architects Jeju Architects, Seongcheon Ko
Participants & Affiliations: Jeju Special Self-Governing Province

Johannesburg — Shifting Borders and Building Bridges
Curators: Alexandra Parker
Participants & Affiliations: Gauteng City-Region Observatory, Gauteng Provincial Government, South African Local Government Association, University of Johannesburg (UJ), University of the Witwatersrand, Eben Keun (Chief

Brand Architect), Hester Viljoen (Project Manager)

London — London Made
Curators: We Made That
Participants & Affiliations: Mayor of London (Alex Marsh, Project leader), British Council, New London Architecture, SEGRO, Barbican Centre (Featured Cultural Venue), Alice Masters (Film Director), Joe Almond (Assistant Camera), Dan Hayhurst (Sound Editor), Maddison Graphic (Graphic Design)

London, Annex — Place, Spaces, Work
Curators: Publica, The Store Studios, 180 The Strand

Macao — Macao Shaped by Use: Formalizing the Vernacular Customization of the City
Curators: Nuno Soares, Filipa Simões

Madrid — DREAMadrid
Curators: Jose Luis Esteban Penelas, James London Mills, Santiago Porras Alvarez, Daniel Valle Almagro, Maria Esteban Casanas
Participants & Affiliations: COAM Official Chamber of Architects of Madrid, Universidad Europea de Madrid, UEM, Ayuntamiento de Madrid (Municipality of Madrid), AIR LAB Architectural International Research Laboratory Design Institute, Grupo Tecma Red S.L., Carto

Medellín — A City for Life
Curators: Jorge Perez Jaramillo
Participants & Affiliations: Sebastian Monsalve (Co-Curator, Design Production), Gioranna Spera, Corporation Amigos Parques Delrio, Horacio Valencia, Carlos Pordo

Messina — Messina Waterfront Polycenter: A Socio Economic and Cultural Catalyst
Curators: Claudio Lucchesi
Participants & Affiliations: Urban Future Organization, Andrew Yau (Curator), Renato Accorinti (Mayor of Messina)

Mexico City — A Living Laboratory to Prototype: The Future of the Cities We Want
Curators: Gabriella Gomez Mont
Participants & Affiliations: Laboratorio para la Ciudad, Clorinda Romo (Director of Creative Projects at Laboratory for the City), Alejandro Ruiz (Head of

Design at Laboratory for the City)

Mumbai — The Bench-Ladder Conversations: Between Systems and Madness
Curators: Rupali Gupte, Prasad Shetty (BARD Studio)
Participants & Affiliations: Vinit Dharia (Project Assistant)

Oslo — Edible Oslo
Curators: Øystein Rø, Espen Røyseland
Participants & Affiliations: Transborder Studio, Soyoung Lee (Illustration)

Paris — *Réinventer* Paris
Curators: Pavillon de l'Arsenal

Pyongyang — Pyongyang Sallim
Curators: Dongwoo Yim, Calvin Chua

Reykjavík — The Hot Pot as Political Arena
Curators: Arna Mathiesen
Participants & Affiliations: April Arkitekter, Harpa Fönn Sigurjónsdóttir (Film), Kjersti Hembre, Kathrine Lagethon Lunøe (Design), Brynja Baldursdóttir (Graphic), Thomas Forget (Text), Anna Maria Bogadóttir (Media)

Rome — The Theaters of Culture: Ephemeral Projects for the Eternal City
Curators: Pippo Ciorra
Participants & Affiliations: MAXXI, Future Architecture Platform, Comune di Roma, Luca Galofaro (Curator and Exhibition Designer), Alessandra Spagnoli (General Coordinator)

San Francisco — At Home Together
Curators: Neeraj Bhatia, Antje Steinmuller
Participants & Affiliations: Urban Works Agency

São Paulo — Food Circuit in São Paulo
Curators: Denise Xavier de Mendonça, Anderson Kazuo Nakano, Antonio Rodriges Netto
Participants & Affiliations: Centro Universitário Belas Artes de São Paulo

Sejong — Zero-Energy Smart City Development
Curators: National Agency for Administrative City Construction

Seoul — Sectioning Seoul
Curators: Sora Kim
Participants & Affiliations: Seoul Metropolitan Government, Junha Jeon (Assistant Curator), 05Studio (Assistant Curator)

Seoul, Seongbuk — Seongbuk Art Commons
Curators: Youjoung Jang (Curator), Woonkie Kim (Co-Curator), Jang-Oh Hong (Co-Curator)
Participants & Affiliations: Mijeong Kim (Assistant Curator), Nanyong Kim (Assistant Curator)

SH Corporation — Seoul Housing and Community Movements 1: Towards Open Communities
Curators: Jieun Kim, Taejin Lee, Gyeongoh Chung
Participants & Affiliations: Seoul Housing & Communities Corporation, Sora Kim

SH Corporation — Seoul Housing and Community Movements 2: Landscripts for New Communities: Seoul via Vienna
Curators: Hae-Won Shin
Participants & Affiliations: Seoul Housing and Communities Corporation, Mladen Jadric

Shanghai — The Other Factory: Late-Industrial Organization and Form
Curators: H. Koon Wee, Eunice M. F. Seng, Darren X Zhou
Participants & Affiliations: SKEW Collaborative

Shenzhen—Shenzhen to PRD Method
Curators: Jason Hilgefort, Merve Bedir (Future+Aformal Academy)

Singapore — White Space
Curators: Keng Hua Chong, Calvin Chua You Jin
Participants & Affiliations: Singapore University of Technology and Design (SUTD)

Sydney — Spatial Frameworks: City Strategy in the Twenty-first Century
Curators: Gerard Reinmuth
Participants & Affiliations: University of Technology, Sydney, Government Architect NSW, Kim Denise Ohrstrom, Maria Luisa Vittorelli (Exhibition design)

Tehran — Cultivating Tehran
Curators: Amin Tadjsoleiman
Participants & Affiliations: Tehran Urban Innovation Center (TUIC), Nashid Nabian (Designer), Shima Roshanzamir (Designer)

Tijuana / San Diego — Living Borders
Curators: Rene Peralta
Participants & Affiliations: Instituto Metropolitano de Planeacion de Tijuana, BC. Mexico, San Diego State University, El Colegio de la Frontera Norte, Denise Luna (Designer), Alejandro Santander (Designer)

Tokyo — Common Matters
Curators: Keigo Kobayashi, Christian Dimmer
Participants & Affiliations: Waseda University

Vienna — The Vienna Model
Curators: Wolfgang Förster
Participants & Affiliations: IBA Vienna

Yeongju — Multiple System of Urban-Rural Integrated City: Yeongju's Public Architecture Masterplan
Curators: Urban Affairs Division, Yeongju City
Participants & Affiliations: Space Magazine

Cityscape — Homo Urbanus
Curators: Bêka and Lemoine
Participants & Affiliations: Agora Biennale de Bordeaux

Toward a (Dis)-Educating City: The (Dis)-Educational Workshop
Curators: Giuseppe Stampone
Participants & Affiliations: MLF I Marie-Laure Fleisch

Cities and Communities — A Three-Way Dialogue
Curators: Space One, Inyoung Yeo

Urban Patterns — Emergent Tokyo: Five Spontaneous Urban Patterns
Curators: Keio University Almazán Lab

SEOUL BIENNALE OF ARCHITECTURE AND URBANISM 2017: IMMINENT COMMONS

HOSTED BY
Seoul Metropolitan Government
Seoul Design Foundation

Directors
Hyungmin Pai
Alejandro Zaera-Polo

GENERAL MANAGER
Soik Jung

PROJECT MANAGERS
Nayeon Kim
Hye Seong Park
Myungcheol Shin
Myeongju Keum
Suna Lee
Green Kim
Ri Jin Yoo
Jina Lee
Sunjae Kim
Sobaek Oh

IMMINENT COMMONS: COMMONING CITIES

First published by
Seoul Biennale of Architecture and Urbanism, Actar Publishers, 2017

EDITED BY
Helen Hejung Choi, Hyungmin Pai

With the Collaboration of
Hyoeun Kim, Donghwa Kang, Dasom Gong, Ri Jin Yoo

TRANSLATED BY
Translation Cooperative (Nam Sunok), Kim Yong-bom, Kyunghee Lee

PROOF-READING
MaryNeal Meador
Helen Elizabeth Gyger
Hyungmin Pai

COPY-EDITING
Anthony Findley

TRANSLATION AND EDITING COORDINATION
Kyunghee Lee (khlmiis@gmail.com)
Dasom Gong (gongda0608@gmail.com)

GRAPHIC IDENTITY AND DUST JACKET DESIGN
Sulki & Min

GRAPHIC DESIGN OF THE BOOK
Workroom

PRINTED, BINDED BY
Intime

COPYRIGHT
© 2017 Seoul Biennale of Architecture and Urbanism, Actar Publishers
© Texts and images by the authors

DISTRIBUTED BY
Actar Publishers
440 Park avenue South, 17th Floor
New York, NY 10016
T +1 212 966 2207
F +1 212 966 2214
salesnewyork@actar-d.com

Barcelona
Roca I Batlle 2-4
08023 Barcelona
T +34 933 282 183
salesbarcelona@actar-d.com
eurosales@actar-d.com

ISBN 978-1-945150-66-1
Library of Congress Control Number: 2017952491
A CIP catalogue record for this book is available from the Library of Congress, Washington D.C., U.S.A.

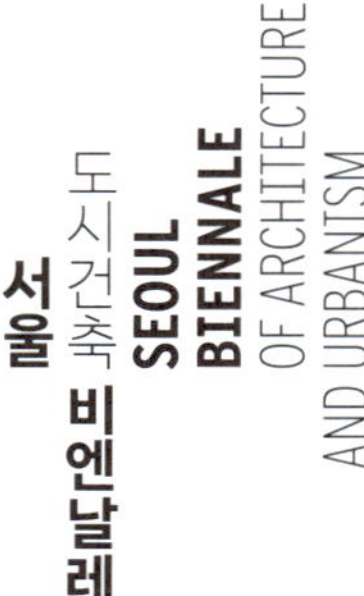